BOSTON, 135 WASHINGTON STREET,
APRIL, 1853.

NEW BOOKS AND NEW EDITIONS

PUBLISHED BY

TICKNOR, REED, AND FIELDS.

THOMAS DE QUINCEY'S WRITINGS.

CONFESSIONS OF AN ENGLISH OPIUM-EATER, AND SUSPIRIA DE PROFUNDIS. With Portrait. Price 75 cents.

BIOGRAPHICAL ESSAYS. Price 75 cents.

MISCELLANEOUS ESSAYS. Price 75 cents.

THE CÆSARS. Price 75 cents.

LIFE AND MANNERS. Price 75 cents.

LITERARY REMINISCENCES. 2 Vols. Price $1.50.

NARRATIVE AND MISCELLANEOUS PAPERS. 2 Vols. Price $1 50.

ESSAYS ON THE POETS, &c. 1 vol. 16mo. 75 cents.

HISTORICAL AND CRITICAL ESSAYS. 2 vols. Price $1.50.

ALFRED TENNYSON'S WRITINGS.

POETICAL WORKS. With Portrait. 2 vols. Boards. $1.50.

THE PRINCESS. Boards. Price 50 cents.

IN MEMORIAM. Cloth. Price 75 cents.

BARRY CORNWALL'S WRITINGS.

ENGLISH SONGS AND OTHER SMALL POEMS. Enlarged Edition. Price $1.00.

ESSAYS AND TALES IN PROSE. 2 Vols. Price $1.50.

HENRY W. LONGFELLOW'S WRITINGS.

THE GOLDEN LEGEND. A Poem. Just Published. Price $1.00.

POETICAL WORKS. This edition contains the six Volumes mentioned below. In two volumes. 16mo. Boards. $2.00.

In separate Volumes, each 75 cents.

VOICES OF THE NIGHT.

BALLADS AND OTHER POEMS.

SPANISH STUDENT; A PLAY IN THREE ACTS.

BELFRY OF BRUGES, AND OTHER POEMS.

EVANGELINE; A TALE OF ACADIE.

THE SEASIDE AND THE FIRESIDE.

THE WAIF. A Collection of Poems. Edited by Longfellow.

THE ESTRAY. A Collection of Poems. Edited by Longfellow.

MR. LONGFELLOW'S PROSE WORKS.

HYPERION. A ROMANCE. Price $1.00.

OUTRE-MER. A PILGRIMAGE. Price $1.00.

KAVANAGH. A TALE. Price 75 cents.

Illustrated editions of THE POEMS and HYPERION.

NATHANIEL HAWTHORNE'S WRITINGS.

TWICE-TOLD TALES. Two Volumes. Price $1.50.

THE SCARLET LETTER. Price 75 cents.

THE HOUSE OF THE SEVEN GABLES. Price $1.00.

THE SNOW IMAGE, AND OTHER TWICE-TOLD TALES. Price 75 cents.

THE BLITHEDALE ROMANCE. Price 75 cents.

TRUE STORIES FROM HISTORY AND BIOGRAPHY. With four fine Engravings. Price 75 cents.

A WONDER-BOOK FOR GIRLS AND BOYS. With seven fine Engravings. Price 75 cents.

TANGLEWOOD TALES. Another "Wonder-Book." In press.

JOHN G. WHITTIER'S WRITINGS.

OLD PORTRAITS AND MOD. SKETCHES. Price 75 cents.

MARGARET SMITH'S JOURNAL. Price 75 cents.

SONGS OF LABOR, AND OTHER POEMS. Boards. 50 cts.

THE CHAPEL OF THE HERMITS. Cloth. 50 cents.

JAMES RUSSELL LOWELL'S WRITINGS.

COMPLETE POETICAL WORKS. Revised, with Additions. In two volumes, 16mo. Boards. Price $1.50.

SIR LAUNFAL. New Edition. Price 25 cents.

THE BIGLOW PAPERS. A New Edition. Price 63 cents.

EDWIN P. WHIPPLE'S WRITINGS.

ESSAYS AND REVIEWS. 2 Vols. Price $2.00.

LECTURES ON SUBJECTS CONNECTED WITH LITERATURE AND LIFE. Price 63 cents.

WASHINGTON AND THE REVOLUTION. Price 20 cts.

OLIVER WENDELL HOLMES'S WRITINGS.

POETICAL WORKS. With fine Portrait. Boards. $1.00.

ASTRÆA. Fancy paper. Price 25 cents.

GRACE GREENWOOD'S WRITINGS.

GREENWOOD LEAVES. 1st & 2d Series. $1.25 each.

POETICAL WORKS. With fine Portrait. Price 75 cents.

HISTORY OF MY PETS. With six fine Engravings. Scarlet cloth. Price 50 cents.

RECOLLECTIONS OF MY CHILDHOOD. With six fine Engravings. Scarlet cloth. Price 50 cents.

MRS. JUDSON'S WRITINGS.

ALDERBROOK. By Fanny Forester. 2 Vols. Price $1.75

THE KATHAYAN SLAVE, AND OTHER PAPERS. 1 vol. Price 63 cents.

HENRY GILES'S WRITINGS.

LECTURES, ESSAYS, AND MISCELLANEOUS WRITINGS. 2 Vols. Price $1.50.

DISCOURSES ON LIFE. Price 75 cents.

R. H. STODDARD'S WRITINGS.

POEMS. Cloth. Price 63 cents.

ADVENTURES IN FAIRY LAND. Just out. 75 cents.

WILLIAM MOTHERWELL'S WRITINGS.

POEMS, NARRATIVE AND LYRICAL. New Ed. $1.25.

POSTHUMOUS POEMS. Boards. Price 50 cents.

MINSTRELSY, ANC. AND MOD. 2 Vols. Boards. $1.50.

GOETHE'S WRITINGS.

WILHELM MEISTER. Translated by Thomas Carlyle. 2 Vols. Price $2.50.

GOETHE'S FAUST. Translated by Hayward. Price 75 cts.

MRS. CROSLAND'S WRITINGS.

LYDIA: A WOMAN'S BOOK. Cloth. 75 cents.

ENGLISH TALES AND SKETCHES. Cloth. $1.00.

MISCELLANEOUS.

CHARLES MACKAY'S POEMS. 1 Vol. Cloth. Price $1.00.

ROBERT BROWNING'S Poetical Works. 2 Vols. $2.00.

HENRY ALFORD'S POEMS. Just out. Price $1.25.

RICHARD MONCKTON MILNES. Poems of Many Years. Boards. Price 75 cents.

CHARLES SPRAGUE. Poetical and Prose Writings. With fine Portrait. Boards. Price 75 cents.

BAYARD TAYLOR. Poems. Cloth. Price 63 cents.

HENRY T. TUCKERMAN. Poems. Cloth. Price 75 cents.

JOHN G. SAXE. Poems. With Portrait. Boards, 63 cents. Cloth, 75 cents.

BOWRING'S MATINS AND VESPERS. Price 50 cents.

REJECTED ADDRESSES. By Horace and James Smith. Boards, Price 50 cents. Cloth, 63 cents.

WARRENIANA. A Companion to the 'Rejected Addresses.' Price 63 cents.

MEMORY AND HOPE. A Book of Poems, referring to Childhood. Cloth. Price $2.00.

JOSEPH T. BUCKINGHAM'S PERSONAL MEMOIRS AND RECOLLECTIONS OF EDITORIAL LIFE. With Portrait. 2 vols. 16mo. Price $1.50.

VILLAGE LIFE IN EGYPT. By the Author of 'Adventures in the Lybian Desert.' 2 vols. 16mo. Price $1.25.

PALISSY THE POTTER. By the Author of 'How to make Home Unhealthy.' 2 vols. 16mo. Price $1.50.

WILLIAM MOUNTFORD. Thorpe: A Quiet English Town, and Human Life therein. 16mo. Price $1.00.

JAMES FREEMAN CLARKE. Eleven Weeks in Europe, and what may be seen in that time. 16mo. Price $1.00.

CAPT. MAYNE REID. THE DESERT HOME, OR THE ADVENTURES OF A LOST FAMILY IN THE WILDERNESS. 12 Engravings. 16mo. Price $1.00.

THE BOY HUNTERS. By the Author of 'The Desert Home.' Price 75 cents.

WILLIAM WORDSWORTH'S BIOGRAPHY. By Dr. C. WORDSWORTH. 2 Vols. Price $2.50.

MRS. A. C. LOWELL. THOUGHTS ON THE EDUCATION OF GIRLS. Price 25 cents.

CHARLES SUMNER. ORATIONS AND SPEECHES. 2 Vols. Price $2.50.

GEORGE S. HILLARD. THE DANGERS AND DUTIES OF THE MERCANTILE PROFESSION. Price 25 cents.

HORACE MANN. A FEW THOUGHTS FOR A YOUNG MAN. Price 25 cents.

F. W. P. GREENWOOD. SERMONS OF CONSOLATION. $1.00.

HEROINES OF THE MISSIONARY ENTERPRISE. 75 cts.

MEMOIR OF THE BUCKMINSTERS, FATHER AND SON. By Mrs. LEE. Price $1.25.

THE SOLITARY OF JUAN FERNANDEZ. By the Author of Picciola. Price 50 cents.

THE BOSTON BOOK. Price $1.25.

ANGEL-VOICES. Price 38 cents.

FLORENCE, AND OTHER TALES. By Mrs. LEE. 50 cts.

SIR ROGER DE COVERLEY. From the 'Spectator.' Price 75 cents.

S. T. WALLIS. SPAIN, HER INSTITUTIONS, POLITICS, AND PUBLIC MEN. Price $1.00.

RUTH, A New Novel by the Author of 'MARY BARTON.' Price 75 cents.

LABOR AND LOVE: A TALE OF ENGLISH LIFE. 50 cents.

EACH OF THE ABOVE POEMS AND PROSE WRITINGS, MAY BE HAD IN VARIOUS STYLES OF HANDSOME BINDING.

JUVENILE.

GRACE GREENWOOD'S

HISTORY OF MY PETS. A new and beautiful book, with six fine engravings. Square 16mo. Scarlet cloth, 50 cents.

RECOLLECTIONS OF MY CHILDHOOD. 50 cents.

NATHANIEL HAWTHORNE'S

TRUE STORIES FROM HISTORY AND BIOGRAPHY. With engravings. 16mo. Cloth gilt, 75 cents; cloth, gilt edge, $1.00.

WONDER-BOOK FOR GIRLS AND BOYS. With Engravings. 1 vol. 16mo. Cloth gilt, 75 cents; cloth, gilt edge, $1.00.

ADVENTURES IN FAIRY LAND. By R. H. Stoddard. With fine plates. Just out. Price 75 cents.

AUNT EFFIE'S RHYMES. With beautiful Engravings. Just published. 75 cents.

ELIZA BUCKMINSTER LEE. Florence, The Parish Orphan; and A Sketch of The Village in the Last Century. 1 vol. 16mo. Cloth, 50 cents; cloth, gilt edge, 63 cents.

MRS. SARAH P. DOUGHTY. The Little Child's Friend. With illustrations. 1 vol. square 16mo. Cloth, 38 cents.

MEMOIRS OF A LONDON DOLL. Written by herself. Edited by Mrs. Fairstair. With engravings. 1 vol. square 16mo. Scarlet cloth, 50 cents; gilt edge, 63 cents.

THE DESERT HOME, or, The Adventures of a Lost Family in the Wilderness. By Capt. Mayne Reid. With fine plates, $1.00.

THE BOY HUNTERS. By Capt. Reid. With fine plates. Just published.

TALES FROM CATLAND, for Little Kittens. By an Old Tabby. With engravings. 1 vol. square 16mo. Scarlet cloth, 50 cents; gilt edge, 63 cents.

THE DOLL AND HER FRIENDS; A Companion to the 'Memoirs of a London Doll.' With illustrations. 1 vol. square 16mo., 50 cents.

MRS. BARBAULD'S LESSONS FOR CHILDREN. With engravings. 16mo. Cloth, 40 cents.

JACOB ABBOTT'S JONAS'S STORIES. Related to Rollo and Lucy. 18mo. Cloth, 38 cents.

JONAS A JUDGE; or Law among the Boys. Cloth, 38 cents.

JONAS ON A FARM IN SUMMER. Cloth, 38 cents.

JONAS ON A FARM IN WINTER. Cloth, 38 cents.

The Same in two vols., red cloth, gilt, $1.50

JACK HALLIARD. Voyages and Adventures in the Arctic Ocean. With Engravings. 16mo. Cloth, 38 cents.

S. G. GOODRICH'S

LAMBERT LILLY'S HISTORY OF THE NEW-ENGLAND States. With numerous Engravings. 18mo. Cloth, 38 cts.

LAMBERT LILLY'S HISTORY OF THE MIDDLE STATES. With numerous Engravings. 18mo. Cloth, 38 cents.

LAMBERT LILLY'S HISTORY of the SOUTHERN STATES: Virginia, North and South Carolina, and Georgia. With numerous Engravings. 18mo. Cloth, 38 cents.

LAMBERT LILLY's HISTORY of the WESTERN STATES. With numerous Engravings. 18mo. Cloth, 38 cents.

LAMBERT LILLY'S STORY OF THE AMERICAN REVOLUTION. With numerous Engravings. 18mo. Cloth, 38 cents.

THE SAME, in 3 Vols. Red cloth, gilt, $1.88.

MARY HOWITT'S Birds and Flowers, and other Country Things. With Engravings. 12mo. 50 cents.

PARLEY'S Short Stories for Long Nights. With eight colored Engravings, 16mo. cloth, 50 cents; uncolored Engravings, 40 cents.

PARLEY'S SMALL PICTURE BOOKS. With colored Frontispieces, printed covers. 16mo. Eight kinds, assorted. Per gross, $9.00.

THE DUCKS AND THE FROGS. With Engravings from Designs by Billings. 13 cents.

THE INDESTRUCTIBLE BOOKS FOR CHILDREN. Printed on strong Cloth, expressly prepared. Four kinds, viz.: Alphabet — Primer — Spelling Book — Reading Book. Each 25 cents.

THE FOUR PARTS, Bound in one Cloth volume, 90 Pictures, $1.25.

THE

KATHAYAN SLAVE,

AND

OTHER PAPERS

CONNECTED WITH MISSIONARY LIFE.

BY

EMILY JUDSON.

BOSTON:
TICKNOR, REED, AND FIELDS.
MDCCCLIII.

THURSTON, TORRY, AND EMERSON, PRINTERS.

TO THE

REV. FRANCIS WAYLAND, D. D.,

WHOSE ETHICS MINGLED LARGELY IN THE DISCIPLINARY INFLUENCES OF MY SCHOOL-DAYS; WHOSE INSPIRITING, LIFE-ENNOBLING THEOLOGY CHEERED ME THROUGH SOME TANGLED PASSES, IN MATURER YEARS; AND TO WHOSE RECENT FRIENDSHIP I AM INDEBTED FOR MANY A SILVER BORDER TO THE CLOUDS OF SORROW,

THIS LITTLE VOLUME

IS RESPECTFULLY AND MOST GRATEFULLY INSCRIBED,

BY

EMILY JUDSON.

CONTENTS

THE KATHAYAN SLAVE.

At the commencement of the English and Burmese war of 1824, all the Christians (called 'hat-wearers,' in contradistinction from the turbaned heads of the Orientals) residing at Ava, were thrown unceremoniously into the Death-prison. Among them were both Protestant and Roman Catholic missionaries; some few reputable European traders; and criminals shadowed from the laws of Christendom 'under the sole of the golden foot.' These, Americans, English, Spanish, Portuguese, Greek and Armenian, were all huddled together in one prison, with villains of every grade, — the thief, the assassin, the bandit, or all three in one; constituting, in connection with countless other crimes, a blacker character than the inhabitant of a civilized land can picture. Sometimes stript of their clothing, sometimes nearly starved, loaded with heavy irons, thrust into a hot, filthy, noisome apartment, with criminals for companions and criminals for guards, compelled to see the daily torture, to hear the shriek of anguish from writhing victims, with death, death in some terribly detestable form, always before them, a severer state of suffering can scarcely be imagined.

The Burmese had never been known to spare the lives of their war-captives; and though the little band of foreigners could scarcely be called prisoners of war, yet this well-known custom, together with their having been thrust into the death-prison, from which there was no escape, except by a pardon from the king, cut off nearly every reasonable hope of rescue. But, (quite a new thing in the annals of Burmese history,) although some died from the intensity of their sufferings, no foreigner was wantonly put to death. Of those who were claimed by the English at the close of the war, some one or two are yet living, with anklets and bracelets which they will carry to the grave with them, wrought in their flesh by the heavy iron. It may well be imagined, that these men might unfold to us scenes of horror, incidents daily occurring under their own shuddering gaze, in comparison with which the hair-elevating legends of Ann Radcliff would become simple fairy tales.

The death-prison at Ava was at that time a single large room, built of rough boards, without either window or door, and with but a thinly thatched roof to protect the wretched inmates from the blaze of a tropical sun. It was entered by slipping aside a single board, which constituted a sort of sliding-door. Around the prison, inside the yard, were ranged the huts of the under-jailers, or *Children of the Prison*, and outside of the yard, close at hand, that of the head-jailer. These jailers must necessarily be condemned criminals, with a ring, the sign of outlawry, traced in the skin of the cheek, and the name of their crime engraved in the same manner upon the breast. The head-jailer was a tall, bony man, with sinews of iron; wearing, when speaking, a malicious smirk, and given at times to a most revolting kind of jocoseness. When silent and quiet, he had a jaded, care-worn look; but it was at the torture that he was in his proper element. Then his face lighted up—became glad, furious, demoniac. His small black eyes glittered like those of a serpent; his thin lips rolled back, displaying his toothless gums in front, with a long, protruding tusk on either side, stained black as ebony; his hollow, ringed cheeks seemed to contract more and more, and his breast heaved with convulsive delight beneath the fearful word—MAN-KILLER. The prisoners called him *father*, when he was present to enforce this expression of affectionate familiarity; but among themselves he was irreverently christened the *Tiger-cat.*

One of the most active of the Children of the Prison, was a short, broad-faced man, labelled THIEF, who, as well as the Tiger, had a peculiar talent in the way of torturing; and so fond was he of the use of the whip, that he often missed his count, and zealously exceeded the number of lashes ordered by the city governor. The wife of this man was a most odious creature, filthy, bold, impudent, cruel, and like her husband, delighting in torture. Her face was not only deeply pitted with small-pox, but so deformed with leprosy, that the white cartilage of the nose was laid entirely bare; from her large mouth shone rows of irregular teeth, black as ink; her hair, which was left entirely to the care of nature, was matted in large black masses about her head; and her manner, under all this hideous ugliness, was insolent and vicious. They had two children — little vipers, well loaded with venom; and by their vexatious mode of annoyance, trying the tempers of the prisoners more than was in the power of the mature torturers.

As will readily be perceived, the security of this prison was not in the strength of the structure, but in the heavy manacles, and the living wall. The lives of the jailers depended entirely on their fidelity; and fidelity involved strict obedience to orders, however ferocious. As for themselves, they could not escape; they had nowhere to go; certain death awaited them everywhere, for they bore on cheek and breast the ineffaceable proof of their outlawry. Their only safety was at their post; and there was no safety there in humanity, even if it were possible for such degraded creatures to have a spark of humanity left. So inclination united with interest to make them what they really were — demons.

The arrival of a new prisoner was an incident calculated to excite but little interest in the hat-wearers, provided he came in turban and waistcloth. But one morning, there was brought in a young man, speaking the Burmese brokenly, and with the soft accent of the north, who at once attracted universal attention. He was tall and erect, with a mild, handsome face, bearing the impress of inexpressible suffering; a complexion slightly tinted with the rich brown of the east; a fine, manly carriage, and a manner which, even there, was both graceful and dignified.

'Who is he?' was the interpretation of the inquiring glances exchanged among those who had no liberty to speak; and then eye asked of eye, 'What can he have done? — he, so gentle, so mild, so manly, that even these wretches, who scarcely know the name of pity and respect, seem to feel both for him?' There was, in truth, something in the countenance of the new prisoner which, without asking for sympathy, involuntarily enforced it. It was not amiability, though his dark, soft, beautiful eye was full of a noble sweetness; it was not resignation; it was not apathy; it was hopelessness, deep, utter, immovable, suffering hopelessness. Very young, and apparently not ambitious or revengeful, what crime could this interesting stranger have committed to draw down 'the golden foot' with such crushing weight upon his devoted head? He seemed utterly friendless, and without even the means of obtaining food; for, as the day advanced, no one came to see him; and the officer who brought him had left no directions. He did not, however, suffer from this neglect, for Madam Thief, (most wonderful to relate!) actually shared so deeply in the universal sympathy, as to bring him a small quantity of boiled rice and water.

Toward evening, the Woon-bai, a governor, or rather Mayor of the city, entered the prison, his bold, lion-like face as open and unconcerned as ever, but with something of unusual bustling in his manner.

'Where is he?' he cried sternly; 'where is he? this son of Kathay? this dog, villain, traitor! where is he? Aha! only one pair of irons? Put on five! do you hear? five!'

The Woon-bai remained till his orders were executed, and the poor Kathayan was loaded with five pairs of fetters; and then he went out, frowning on one and smiling on another; while the Children of the Prison watched his countenance and manner, as significant of what was expected of them. The prisoners looked at each other, and shook their heads in commiseration.

The next day the feet of the young Kathayan, in obedience to some new order, were placed in the stocks, which raised them about eighteen inches from the ground; and the five pairs of fetters were all disposed on the outer side of the plank, so that their entire weight fell upon the ankles. The position was so painful that each prisoner, some from memory, some from sympathetic apprehension, shared in the pain when he looked at the sufferer.

During this day, one of the missionaries, who had been honored with an invitation, which it was never prudent to refuse, to the hut of the Thief, learned something of the history of the young man, and his crime. His home, it was told him, was among the rich hills of Kathay, as they range far northward, where the tropic sun loses the intense fierceness of his blaze, and makes the atmosphere soft and luxurious, as though it were mellowing beneath the same amber sky which ripens the fruits, and gives their glow to the flowers. What had been his rank in his own land, the jailer's wife did not know. Perhaps he had been a prince, chief of the brave band conquered by the superior force of the Burmans; or a hunter among the spicy groves and deep-wooded jungles, lithe as the tiger which he pursued from lair to lair, and free as the flame-winged bird of the sun that circled above him; or perhaps his destiny had been a humbler one, and he had but followed his goats as they bounded fearlessly from ledge to ledge, and plucked for food the herbs upon his native hills. He had been brought away by a marauding party, and presented as a slave to the brother of the queen. This *Men-thah-gyee*, the Great Prince, as he was called, by way of pre-eminence, had risen, through the influence of his sister, from the humble condition of a fishmonger, to be the Richelieu of the nation. Unpopular from his mean origin, and still more unpopular from the acts of brutality to which the intoxication of power had given rise, the sympathy excited by the poor Kathayan in the breasts of these wretches may easily be accounted for. It was not pity or mercy, but hatred. Anywhere else, the sufferer's sad, handsome face, and mild, uncomplaining manner, would have enlisted sympathy; but here, they would scarcely have seen the sadness, or beauty, or mildness, except through the medium of a passion congenial to their own natures.

Among the other slaves of Men-thah-gyee, was a young Kathay girl of singular beauty. She was, so said Madam the Thief, a bundle of roses, set round with the fragrant blossoms of the champac tree; her breath was like that of the breezes when they come up from their dalliance with the spicy daughters of the islands of the south; her voice had caught its rich cadence from the musical gush of the silver fountain, which wakes among the green of her native hills; her hair had been braided from the glossy raven plumage of the royal edolius; her eyes were twin stars looking out from cool springs, all fringed with the long, tremulous reeds of the jungle; and her step was as the free, graceful bound of the wild antelope. On the subject of her grace, her beauty, and her wondrous daring, the jailer's wife could not be sufficiently eloquent. And so this poor, proud, simple-souled maiden, this diamond from the rich hills of Kathay, destined to glitter for an hour or two on a prince's bosom, unsubdued even in her desolation, had dared to bestow her affections with the uncalculating lavishness of conscious heart-freedom. And the poor wretch, lying upon his back in the death-prison, his feet fast in the stocks and swelling and purpling beneath the heavy irons, had participated in her crime; had lured her on, by tender glances and by loving words, inexpressibly sweet in their mutual bondage, to irretrievable destruction. What fears, what hopes winged by fears, what tremulous joys, still hedged in by that same crowd of fears, what despondency, what revulsions of impotent anger and daring, what weeping, what despair must have been theirs! Their tremblings and rejoicings, their mad projects, growing each day wilder and more dangerous — since madness alone could have given rise to anything like hope — are things left to imagination; for there was none to relate the heart-history of the two slaves of Men-thah-gyee. Yet there were some hints of a first accidental meeting under the shadow of the mango and tamarind trees, where the sun lighted up, by irregular gushes, the waters of the little lake in the centre of the garden, and the rustle of leaves seemed sufficient to drown the accents of their native tongues. So they looked, spoke, their hearts bounded, paused, trembled with soft home-memories — they whispered on, and they were lost. Poor slaves!

Then at evening, when the dark-browed maidens of the golden city, gathered, with their earthen vessels about the well, there, shaded by the thick clumps of bamboo, with the free sky overhead, the green earth beneath, and the songs and laughter of the merry girls ringing in their ears, so like their own home, the home which they had lost forever — oh, what a rare, sweet, dangerous meeting-place for those who should not, and yet must be lovers!

Finally came a day fraught with illimitable consequences; the day when the young slave, not yet admitted to the royal harem, should become more than ever the property of her master. And now deeper grew their agony, more uncontrollable their madness, wilder and more daring their hopes, with every passing moment. Not a man in Ava, but would have told them that escape was impossible; and yet, goaded on by love and despair, they attempted the impossibility. They had countrymen in the city, and, under cover of night, they fled to them. Immediately the minister sent out his myrmidons — they were tracked, captured, and brought back to the palace.

'And what became of the poor girl?' inquired the missionary with much interest.

The woman shuddered, and beneath her scars and the swarthiness of her skin, she became deadly pale.

'There is a cellar, Tsayah,' at last she whispered, still shuddering, 'a deep cellar, that no one has seen, but horrible cries come from it sometimes, and two nights ago, for three hours, three long hours — such shrieks! Amai-ai!

what shrieks! And they say that he was there, Tsayah, and saw and heard it all. That is the reason that his eyes are blinded and his ears benumbed. A great many go into that cellar, but none ever come out again — none but the doomed like him. It is — *it is like the West Prison*,' she added, sinking her voice still lower, and casting an eager alarmed look about her. The missionary too shuddered, as much at the mention of this prison, as at the recital of the woman; for it shut within its walls deep mysteries, which even his jailers, accustomed as they were to torture and death, shrank from babbling of.

The next day a cord was passed around the wrists of the young Kathayan, his arms jerked up into a position perpendicular with his prostrate body, and the end of the cord fastened to a beam overhead. Still, though faint from the lack of food, parched with thirst, and racked with pain, for his feet were swollen and livid, not a murmur of complaint escaped his lips. And yet this patient endurance seemed scarcely the result of fortitude or heroism; an observer would have said that the inner suffering was so great as to render that of the mere physical frame unheeded. There was the same expression of hopelessness, the same unvarying wretchedness, too deep, too real, to think of giving itself utterance on the face as at his first entrance into the prison; and except that he now and then fixed on one of the hopeless beings who regarded him in silent pity, a mournful, half-beseeching, half-vacant stare, this was all.

That day passed away as others had done; then came another night of dreams, in which loved ones gathered around the hearth-stone of a dear, distant home; dreams broken by the clanking of chains, and the groans of the suffering; and then morning broke. There still hung the poor Kathayan; his face slightly distorted with the agony he was suffering, his lips dry and parched, his cheek pallid and sunken, and his eyes wild and glaring. His breast swelled and heaved, and now and then a sob-like sigh burst forth involuntarily. When the Tiger entered, the eye of the young man immediately fastened on him, and a shiver passed through his frame. The old murderer went his usual rounds with great nonchalance; gave an order here, a blow there, and cracked a malicious joke with a third; smiling all the time that dark, sinister smile, which made him so much more hideous in the midst of his wickedness. At last he approached the Kathayan, who, with a convulsive movement, half raised himself from the ground at his touch, and seemed to contract like a shrivelled leaf.

'Right! right, my son!' said the old man, chuckling. 'You are expert at helping yourself, to be sure; but then you need assistance. So—so—so!' and giving the cord three successive jerks, he succeeded, by means of his immense strength, in raising the Kathayan so that but the back of his head, as it fell downward, could touch the floor. There was a quick, short crackling of joints, and a groan escaped the prisoner. Another groan followed, and then another—and another—a heaving of the chest, a convulsive shiver, and for a moment he seemed lost. Human hearts glanced heavenward. 'God grant it! Father of mercies, spare him farther agony!' It could not be. Gaspingly came the lost breath back again, quiveringly the soft eyes unclosed; and the young Kathayan captive was fully awake to his misery.

'I cannot die so — I cannot — so slow — so slow — so slow!' Hunger gnawed, thirst burned, fever revelled in his veins; the cord upon his wrists cut to the bone; corruption had already commenced upon his swollen, livid feet; the most frightful, torturing pains distorted his body, and wrung from him, groans and murmurings so pitiful, so harrowing, so full of anguish, that the unwilling listeners could only turn away their heads, or lift their eyes to each other's faces in mute horror. Not a word was exchanged among them — not a lip had power to give it utterance.

'I cannot die so! I cannot die so! I cannot die so!' came the words, at first moaningly, and then prolonged to a terrible howl. And so passed another day, and another night, and still the wretch lived on.

In the midst of their filth and smothering heat, the prisoners awoke from such troubled sleep as they could gain amid these horrors; and those who could, pressed their feverish lips and foreheads to the crevices between the boards, to court the morning breezes. A lady, with a white brow, and a lip whose delicate vermilion had not ripened beneath the skies of India, came with food to her husband. By constant importunity had the beautiful ministering angel gained this holy privilege. Her coming was like a gleam of sunlight — a sudden unfolding of the beauties of this bright earth to one born blind. She performed her usual tender ministry and departed.

Day advanced to its meridian; and once more but now hesitatingly, and as though he dreaded his task, the Tiger drew near the young Kathayan. But the sufferer did not shrink from him as before.

'Quick!' he exclaimed, greedily. 'Quick! give me one hand and the cord, — just a moment, a single moment, — this hand with the cord in it, — and you shall be rid of me forever!'

The Tiger burst into a hideous laugh, his habitual cruelty returning at the sound of his victim's voice.

'Rid of you! not so fast, my son; not so fast! You will hold out a day or two yet. Let me see!' passing his hand along the emaciated, feverish body of the sufferer. 'Oh, yes; two days at least, perhaps three, and it may be longer. Patience, my son; you are frightfully strong! Now these joints — why any other man's would have separated long ago; but here they stay just as firmly —' As he spoke with a calculating sort of deliberation, the monster gave the cord a sudden jerk, then another, and a third, raising his victim still farther from the floor, and then adjusting it about the beam, walked unconcernedly away. For several minutes the prison rung with the most fearful cries. Shriek followed shriek, agonized, furious, with scarcely a breath between; bellowings, howlings, gnashings of the teeth, sharp, piercing screams, yells of savage defiance; cry upon cry, cry upon cry, with wild superhuman strength, they came; while the prisoners shrank in awe and terror, trembling in their chains. But this violence soon exhasted itself, and the paroxysm passed, giving place to low, sad moans, irresistibly pitiful. This was a day never to be forgotten, by the hundred wretched creatures congregated in the gloomy death-prison. The sun had never seemed to move so slowly before.

Its setting was gladly welcomed, but yet the night brought no change. Those piteous moans, those agonized groanings seemed no nearer an end than ever.

Another day passed — another night — again day dawned and drew near its close; and yet the poor Kathayan clung to life with frightful tenacity. One of the missionaries, as a peculiar favor, had been allowed to creep into an old shed, opposite the door of the prison; and here he was joined by a companion, just as the day was declining towards evening.

'Oh, will it ever end?' whispered one.

The other only bowed his head between his hands — 'Terrible! terrible!'

'There surely can be nothing worse in the West Prison.'

'Can there be anything worse — can there be more finished demons in the pit?'

Suddenly, while this broken conversation was conducted in a low tone, so as not to draw upon the speakers the indignation of their jailers, they were struck by the singular stillness of the prison. The clanking of chains, the murmur and the groan, the heavy breathing of congregated living beings, the bustle occasioned by the continuous uneasy movement of the restless sufferers, the ceaseless tread of the Children of the Prison, and their bullying voices, all were hushed.

'What is it?' in a lower whisper than ever, and a shaking of the head, and holding their own chains to prevent their rattle, and looks full of wonder, was all that passed between the two listeners. Their amazement was interrupted by a dull, heavy sound, as though a bag of dried bones had been suddenly crushed down by the weight of some powerful foot. Silently they stole to a crevice in the boards, opposite the open door. Not a jailer was to be seen; and the prisoners were motionless and apparently breathless, with the exception of one powerful man, who was just drawing the wooden mallet in his hand for another blow on the temple of the suspended Kathayan. It came down with the same dull, hollow, crushing sound; the body swayed from the point where it was suspended by wrist and ankle, till it seemed that every joint must be dislocated; but the flesh scarcely quivered. The blow was repeated, and then another, and another; but they were not needed. The poor captive Kathayan was dead.

The mallet was placed away from sight, and the daring man hobbled back to his corner, dangling his heavy chain as though it had been a plaything, and striving with all his might to look unconscious and unconcerned. An evident feeling of relief stole over the prisoners; the Children of the Prison came back to their places, one by one, and all went on as before. It was some time before any one appeared to discover the death of the Kathayan. The old Tiger declared it was what he had been expecting, that his living on in this manner was quite out of rule; but that those hardy fellows from the hills never would give in, while there was a possibility of drawing another breath. Then the poor skeleton was unchained, dragged by the heels into the prison-yard, and thrown into a gutter. It did not apparently, fall properly, for one of the jailers altered the position of the shoulders by means of his foot; then clutching the long black hair, jerked the head a little farther on the side. Thus the discolored temple was hidden; and surely that emaciated form gave sufficient evidence of a lingering death. Soon after, a party of government officers visited the prison-yard, touched the corpse with their feet, without raising it; and, apparently satisfied, turned away, as though it had been a dead dog, that they cared not to give farther attention.

Is it strange that, if one were there, with a human heart within him, not brutalized by crime or steeled by passive familiarity with suffering, he should have dragged his heavy chain to the side of the dead, and dropped upon his sharpened, distorted features, the tear, which there was none who had loved him, to shed? Is it strange that tender fingers should have closed the staring eyes, and touched gently the cold brow, which throbbed no longer with pain, and smoothed the frayed hair, and composed the passive limbs decently, though he knew that the next moment rude hands would destroy the result of his pious labor? And is it strange that when all which remained of the poor sufferer, had been jostled into its sackcloth shroud, and crammed down into the dark hole dug for it in the earth, a prayer should have ascended, even from that terrible prison? Not a prayer for the dead; he had received his doom. But an earnest, beseeching, upheaving of the heart, for those wretched beings that, in the face of the pure heavens and the smiling earth, confound, by the inherent blackness of their natures, philosopher, priest or philanthropist, who dares to tickle the ears of the multitude with fair theories of 'Natural religion,' and 'The dignity of human nature.'

MEE SHWAY-EE.[1]

In the tropic land of Burmah,
  Where the sun grows never old;
And the regal-browed palmyra
  Crowns her head with clouds of gold;
On a strange, wild promontory,
  Close beside the rushing sea,
Listening ever to the billows,
  Dwelt poor little Mee Shway-ee.

But along the sandy sea-shore,
  Or amid the foliage green,
Stringing rows of crimson berries,
  Was the maiden never seen;
Never twined she her black tresses
  With the golden mazalee;
For a wild and wo-marked slave-child,
  Was poor little Mee Shway-ee.

[1] A very interesting account of this slave child may be found in the Baptist Missionary Magazine for April, 1829.

And when in the hush of twilight
  Rose a startling eldritch cry,
Answered by the grey-winged osprey,
  Plunging seaward from the sky;
Then the village wives and maidens,
  As they glanced from roof to sea,
Whispered of a human osprey,
  And poor writhing Mee Shway-ee.

But a messenger of Jesus—
  Him who, centuries ago,
Bared His bosom to the arrow
  Winged by human guilt and woe,
And then said, 'Go preach my gospel!
  Lo! I'm evermore with thee;'—
One who served this blessed Jesus,
  Found poor trembling Mee Shway-ee.

Found her wan, and scarred, and bleeding,
  Mad with agony and sin;
So love's arms were opened widely,
  And the sufferer folded in;
Tender fingers soothed and nursed her,
  And 'twas wonderful to see,
How the winning glance of pity
  Tamed the elf-child, Mee Shway-ee.

For, beneath those drooping eyelids
Shone a human spirit now,
And the light of thought came playing
Softly over lip and brow;
But her little footstep faltered, —
Beamed her eye more lovingly, —
And 'twas known that death stood claiming
Gentle, trusting, Mee Shway-ee.

But to her he came an angel,
Throned in clouds of rosy light;
Came to bear her to that Saviour,
Who had broke her weary night;
And with smiles she sought his bosom;
So, beside the rushing sea,
'Neath the weeping casuarina,
Laid they little Mee Shway-ee.

MADNESS OF THE MISSIONARY ENTERPRISE.

'What has been the fruit, or what may reasonably be expected to be the fruit of all these labors and sufferings, of all these privations, sacrifices, sicknesses, and deaths? * * * It is our deliberate conviction that the whole enterprise was uncalled for * * * that she had better have remained at home.' — *Review of Anne Judson's Memoir.* 1828.

'These workings,' [' of brother Carey's mind,'] 'produced a sermon, and the sermon a subscription to convert four hundred and twenty millions of pagans.' — *Edinburgh Review.* 1809.

'So with these 12½ cents a-piece, and a parcel of crazy boys and romantic girls, you are expecting to see the world converted.' — *The Rev. D. B.* 1836.

'The notice of the sailing of Missionaries is too often and speedily followed by the account of their early death; and it is time a word of caution was spoken, especially to females.' — *New York Express.* 1846.

'This is another instance of infatuation,' &c. 'We really think there should be a law against the wholesale sacrifice of life which is continually chronicled among those who imagine they are called to labor in unhealthy climes as the wives of missionaries.' — *Boston Transcript.* 1846.

As I stood not long since in the shadow of the Hopea tree, overlooking the mouldering ashes of one who, in the words of the early Jerusalem Church, had 'hazarded her life for Christ;' and as I thought of all she had suffered, all she had done and dared, the words of her Reviewer rushed upon my mind with almost overpowering force. Boodhistic temples and pagodas still decorate the little promontory on which her grave is made; and monks, with shaven crowns and trailing yellow robes, still promenade the streets, and are reverenced as oracles, by the blinded idolators of Amherst, while all that remains to tell of her, is this grassy mound, and this mildewed, mossy marble.

And may it not, after all, be true that her sacrifice was vain, — that 'the enterprise was uncalled for,' — 'that she had better have remained at home?'

This apparently calm view of the subject, is not the 'deliberate conviction' of one man only, nor of one class of men; but thousands, both in Europe and America, have arrived at similar conclusions. The learned philosopher of Edinburgh, the obscure Baptist preacher, taking an indignant farewell of his mission-tinctured flock, the observant, worldly-wise gentleman of the Express, and the lady editor of Puritanic New England, all join their voices with the Unitarian Reviewer's, and conspire to proclaim that she and all her successors are fanatics, and that the cause in which she fell is based upon the most extravagant absurdity. And, candidly, viewing this subject in the subdued light of sober common sense, have they not good ground for their opinion? Who are the originators, who the supporters of this scheme of modern missions, and what are their plans and resources? Is it headed by some mighty potentate, with the lives and treasure of a nation at his control, and can it display a goodly list of titled names — men of renown, and influence, and power? Was it originated by some deep-judging, far-seeing statesman, whose matchless policy has been the wonder of the age in which he lives? Or did it emanate from some school of reverend sages, so wise, so good, and so philanthropic, as to hold the entire world in awe? Perhaps it has somehow linked itself with commercial interests, and may claim as its projectors those 'merchant princes' who are said to constitute the ballast of the nations, and whose resources are bounded only by the impossibilities of art. Alas no! none of these. Leaving out of the account, as irrelevant to our present purpose, certain stirrings on the continent of Europe all through the eighteenth century, let us take note of the movement among people of our own blood and language. In England it emanated (so says the Edinburgh Review) from a 'nest of consecrated cobblers;' and then a half dozen American school-boys rushed forward to light their tiny tapers at the cobbler's fire. And what was to be done? What Quixotic expedition did these ignorant mechanics and 'crazy boys and girls' contemplate? Nothing less than the entire renovation of the entire world. So, in order to accomplish this magnificent scheme, did they band together, unite all their little resources, and pour their consecrated strength upon a single point? Far from it. Defying all the rules that have ever governed the operations of wise men, they scattered themselves as widely as possible, and the plains of India, Chin-India, and China, the burning deserts of Africa, the frozen, rugged wildernesses of America, and the far Islands of the sea have not been thought too wide a range for these victims of unmitigated madness.

Let us contemplate for a moment one of these fanatics, with his white face and outré garb, sitting down in a strange city, ignorant of the language and customs of the people; yet with the deliberate and avowed intention of subverting their favorite tastes, thwarting their dearest prejudices, overthrowing their time-honored institutions, degrading the memories of their fathers, and teaching them and their sons to worship a God of whom they never before heard, and look forward to an eternity whose very blissfulness is distasteful to them. But this is not all. If he aimed at an outward change merely, his very insanity might be turned to account, and he might wield the power of Lady Hester Stanhope through similar inspiration. The juggler's gown and wand, a charmed necklace, or even the crucifix and rosary of the Romanists would doubtless prove powerful instruments in cunning hands. But no; he has no peculiar dress, no relics, no pretended charms; and he labors not merely for change of *profession*, but the burden of his cry is, 'Ye must be born again!' Every individual, man, woman, and child, must undergo a radical change of nature, a mystic inner renovation, which the teacher himself does not profess ability to compass, and of which he can give no description satisfactory to reason, or more definite in its accuracy, than would be an account of the wanderings of the wind.

But there must be power, somewhere; there must be resources of some sort; otherwise, infatuation itself would die for want of nourishment. Who are the supporters, the encouragers of this stupendous scheme? Still, the 'cobbler,' the blacksmith, and the day-laborer, act a prominent part; but he must have a weary search, indeed, who would find the names of kings, princes, and nobles. Some men of wealth and influence may be scattered through the ranks, here and there; but the poor of this world are emphatically the patrons of missions. The pale seamstress lays aside her hard-earned pittance of a Saturday evening; the washerwoman forgets not the mission penny before she kneels to thank God that another week of toil has been added to her busy life; and the sad-eyed widow calls her hungry troop of little ones about her, tells them of poor heathen children, until their little hearts are melted, and thus she adds her loaf of bread to the sacred treasury. Persons of ampler means give more, *as each one pleases;* but there is no fountain of wealth, no bank, no system of taxation, no legal claim on any person or body of persons; and, of course, no earthly certainty that the project will be able to maintain itself a single month. The madmen who go to the heathen are utterly at the mercy of the madmen who stay at home. And yet, notwithstanding all this uncertainty, there is scarcely a nook of the wide earth which they have not penetrated; scarcely a forest tree, from the stunted fir of the frozen regions, to the tall palm of the south, whose leaves have not quivered to the sacred airs rising from every village spire of fair America.

But a price has been paid for all this — the price of human lives; and so 'it is time a word of caution was spoken — especially to females.' This is doubtless very kind, — kindly intended, and, perhaps, wisely thought, — but who will vouch for its reception? The self-willed young madcaps, who have heard of missions in their cradles, who have read their Bibles in simple faith, and who have bowed their unquestioning hearts to certain mysterious closet-teachings, at which our man of the world would only smile, will scarcely be so easily controlled. Oh, no; would he blow back the hurricane with his lips, or stay the rushing tide with his palm?

Let us look a little closer into the workings of this insanity. A timid young girl, never before suspected of differing materially from other girls, suddenly rises from the midst of loving brothers and sisters, and announces her intention of going away to the heathen. Calmly and deliberately she proposes a sacrifice of all she is now — of all her future earthly prospects. She proposes nothing less than to abandon the sweet companionship of early friends, to leave the shelter of the paternal wing, voluntarily, and perhaps in the midst of opposition and ridicule, cast off the protection of civilized society and the laws of a Christian land, and go out to lead an almost nomadic life among the vilest and most degraded of the human race. Some encourage, some smile, and others stare; while, in many cases, the dissecting knife of criticism is whetted to a miracle of sharpness. A set of petty philosophers, of whom every country village can furnish its quota — physiognomists, phrenologists, psychologists, and professors of other dreamy nonsense, suddenly become aware of a new object for the exercise of their philanthropic vocation. They scan her features, they measure her head, they guage her intellect, they analyze her affections, they trick out in modern frippery some old moth-eaten theory of mind for her benefit; and then give utterance to profound saws about *romance,* — *love of adventure,* — *desire for distinction,* — *a day of repentance,* — while she, poor thing! scared at such doubtful notoriety, involuntarily places her hand on her throat, apprehensive that she may have been metamorphosed into 'the woman that was going to be hanged.' Well, it is a good beginning of the life she is to lead; and, to the over-sensitive, perhaps is needful.

But how is it with their prophecies? Does repentance come? Is her romance crushed beneath the heavy tread of dull, cold reality? Is her love of adventure tamed by the monotonous routine of a missionary life? Is her desire for distinction superseded by misanthropic disappointment, when no human eye but that of her husband is upon her? Follow her, and we shall see.

Lo! her tread is as light as in the gladsome days of girlhood; her smile is as cheerful, and in its brightness there is a depth of meaning, a richness of expression, that it never possessed before. Behold her seated by her rude table, straining her eager eye to follow the dim tracery of the stylus — not through fields of enchanting lore; not over pages replete with the poetry and romance which she once loved. No; she is intent only on making herself familiar with the arbitrary signs of a difficult, unclassified tongue. See with what interest she watches the swarthy lips of the ignorant barbarian, who thinks he honors her by condescending to be her teacher; trying, meantime, to imitate his uncouth sounds, till her voice grows tremulous, and her cheek pales with exertion. Then follow her to her pillow, and hear her murmur the same difficult words in her unrefreshing sleep. Surely this romance is not like other romance. It is too steady and persevering, too much like that high fixedness of purpose, which constitutes the strength of the strongest manhood; and, in its deathless tenacity, it surpasses even that. Well, she goes on day after day, patiently and toilfully — day after day, as monotonously as the weaver's shuttle; and at last, she has a sentence or two at her command. How full of emotion are her face and voice, as she repeats to every stranger on whom her eye falls, '*There is an eternal God!'* '*There is a way of salvation for sinners!'*

But behold! a change. The miasma of a deadly climate has crept into her veins, and is settling down upon the springs of life. She has the strongest motives for wishing to live, but the stealthy progress of insidious disease has beguiled her too long, and she is dying. Now, perhaps, one desperate effort is made to save her — an effort which comes too late. She is tossing on the ocean, but she speaks from a bed of death. Hear her. 'I have done nothing for Christ; but, thanks to His grace, I have had it in my heart to do; and since He sees fit to call me home, I know it is best. His will be done!' The moments ebb. Her breath grows shorter, and her eye is rapidly glazing. Again she speaks, but the ear must bend low to catch the feeble murmur, —'Tell — tell my mother — I — have never been sorry that I came.'

What inconceivable infatuation! What immeasurable madness, even in death! But the contagion stops not here. In the hush of twilight, a seemingly sacred object is gently and solemnly borne to the deck, lifted over the vessel's side; and thus all that was ever mortal, of that now immortal one, sinks in the unfathomed deep. But the plunge, soft and low as it is, reaches to her far native land, and its echo rings out from hill and valley, from busy town, and forest hamlet, shaping itself into the heartfelt exclamation, 'HERE AM I — SEND ME!' A caution, indeed! and what words can point a sterner caution, than the skeleton finger of Death himself?

Take another instance; for 'the notice of the sailing of missionaries' is not *always* 'followed by the account of their early death.' The missionary wife has survived the acclimating process, has learned to use a foreign tongue, and has made for herself a little nucleus of human love. She has become familiar with toil, and suffering, and want, and insult, but she has survived all; and, though her history may partially be read in the pallid cheek and drooping figure, her eye never glowed with a loftier enthusiasm than now, and her lip never curved to a more soul-beaming soul. Far back in her history, when she was a young and blooming wife, does the tale of her trials begin. Then it was that sickness first came, and though she had scarcely ever noted its form before, love imparted singular skill to her unpractised hand, and she pored over books of medicine, until she grew to be almost learned in her new profession. There was a call from the wilderness, and she smiled the one earthly protector from her side, and stood up, alone and sublime in her helplessness, amid swarms of hostile barbarians. The midnight robber came; the pestilence swept past her; the pupil over whom she had wept and prayed, and for whose welfare she had toiled for weary years, sunk back into apostasy; but her heart never fainted, her hand never wavered. She had still other tears and other prayers, and she longed to pour out all in her Master's service. Her own strength failed. She pressed her hand to her aching side, stifled the groan upon her lip, and toiled on. Death visited the missionary's dwelling. The quivering hands of the mother closed the eyes of her first-born child, wrapped the white robes about it, and crossed the little icy fingers on the bosom, while the father prepared the coffin and the grave, then cast the cold clods upon his darling, and sobbed out the final prayer.

The hour of agony passed, and the childless mother was again at her toil. Another, and perhaps still another blossom drooped before her eyes; while some wild river-bank, or the dark dingle shadowed by jungle-trees, became the depository of her dearest treasures. But she paused not, she faltered not, for the madness nestled in the very core of her heart; and there was One she loved better than children, better than her own life. So on, and still onward, in one unvarying track, she has gone, till now another bitter trial awaits her.

She has a darling boy, the oldest that the grave has left her. She has borne him long upon her bosom, she taught him the accents of his mother tongue, she trained his affections, she watched and guided his budding intellect, feeling herself the only avenue through which it might be enriched; and she loves this priceless jewel of her solitude, as no other mother on earth can love. Oh, no; it is not lack of affection, but an intense concentration of all the powers of the soul, strong, deep, ardent, though severely disciplined, that makes her dare the sacrifice. To a casual observer, this son of her watchful loneliness would appear a child of uncommon promise. But the mother knows that this promise is deceitful; that his attainments, quickly and easily made, are superficial; that his seeming intellectuality is not the growth of his own mind, but the result, rather, of a foreign stratum wrought over it; and she trembles lest the hot-house precocity of the child should prove but the precursor of early death, or an imbecile manhood. The thousand stimuli to exertion — especially the invigorating, sharpening contact of mind with mind, peculiar to a civilized people, she has often lamented on her own behalf; and she has, thus far, taxed her ingenuity to the utmost, to prevent her child sinking into the inert listlessness, the inefficiency and indolence, which characterize the heathen character. But she begins to find that it is beyond her power, to impart the mental stamina which he so much needs; while there is nothing in the community surrounding them, to tax his energies, or develope his dormant resources. A physical change, too, is gradually creeping over him. He has grown tall and thin, and there is a sickly stoop in his shoulders. The expression of his face is sad, and disagreeably mature; his features are sharpened; and he has a feeble, timid air, and a querulous tone to his voice, in painful contrast with the freshness and buoyancy suited to his years. The missionary wife and mother has drank many a bitter draught, but there is one before her now, almost too bitter for her to contemplate. She must part from her beloved child, or sacrifice him to maternal weakness. Strange that a bright alternative does not suggest itself. Strange that, as her thoughts revert to her own childhood, the waving grain, the fragrant orchards, the cool, health-inspiring breezes of her native hills, commingled with visions of loved faces, and dear familiar voices, and Sabbath bells, and all the precious associations of early days, should not draw her relenting heart homeward. But, no; the madness is upon her; and a voice is continually proclaiming in her ear, 'He that loveth son or daughter more than me, is not worthy of me.' She takes her child to her bosom for the last time; her last kiss is on his lip, her last prayer is in his ear; the soft, loving pressure of her hand has been left upon his head for the last time; and now she is alone in her agony. It matters not to her that cold cavillers sit in their luxurious mansions, and speculate on the propriety of her sacrifice. She knows that she has the approbation of the eternal God, and to Him alone does she look for consolation, in her sharp anguish.

Years pass, and there is another death-bed. Watch her carefully; listen attentively; see if there come not some little word, some little token of the *repentance* prophesied at the commencement of her career. Threads of silver have begun to mingle with the darker hue shading her temples. She is not old, but she has reached that meridian at which romance usually gives place to maturity of judgment; and her enthusiasm has long since been subjected to the chastening influence of sorrow. Surely she must have gained some wisdom in all these busy years; and perhaps in the mother's last message to her son, she will be able to divest herself of her life-long madness. Let us see. 'Tell him,' she says, 'tell him I have thought of him, and of one more meeting here on earth, with painfully delicious longing. But since it is not the will of God that I should look upon his face again, bid him prepare to meet me hereafter in our Father's mansions. And oh, it is a joy for me to hope, that when I am mouldering in the dust, it may please the Lord to call my son to preach the gospel to these poor heathen!'

What will a word of caution avail against monomaniacy like this? Ah, 'there should be a law.' Indeed! and does not our kind philanthropist know that human invention has been on the rack for the last eighteen centuries to devise a law which should palsy the feet and seal the lips of these same bearers of glad tidings? But we need not go so far back for examples. What but English law caused the early English missionaries to flee to the ships of Denmark and America; and thus spread the contagion of their strange malady far and wide? What but Anglo-Indian law placed the martyr-crown upon the brow of young Harriet Newell; and made every drop of blood that it caused to stagnate in her veins, the germ of another missionary? And what but the same law hunted her companions, like vagabonds, from shore to shore, opening to them new fields of labor, giving the widest possible scope to their powers, and by means of its very hatred of missions, actually planting new missions. And has not the law of every Pagan nation beneath the heavens, from the bloody savages of Sumatra, to the comparatively polished children of the Celestial Empire, closed its strong gates, or shaken its manacles in the face of the unheeding missionary? And what can tolerant America do, more than these? She must have strangely gifted legislators, indeed, to devise an edict that should prove stronger than prison bars and clanking chains; than all the crimson paraphernalia of death, which spreads itself before the missionary in his hour of consecration.

But it is time to inquire what all this wondrous madness means; to search out, if possible, the controlling principle of this mighty progressive movement, which, though begun in obscurity, and carried on in weakness, is rapidly gaining the respect of even the most skeptical. What is it that draws the wisdom of gray hairs, the enthusiasm of youth, and the simplicity of childhood, into a community of feeling and action? What is it that makes the weak strong, the timid daring; that turns the tremulous nerve to iron, and the waxen will to adamant; that laughs alike at human reason and human laws; and goes forth trampling with stern, though meek deliberation, on dangers, difficulties, and death itself? What is it, but the highest, the deepest, the most absorbing principle of our nature — LOVE.

For examples of the strength of this wonder-working principle, in its imperfect human development, we have no need to search occasional records, and take eager note of the wife who follows her husband to the battle-field, or the mother who leaps into the sea, or mounts to the aërie of the eagle, for her child. We have every day before our eyes, in the commonest walks of life, among the rudest natures, beautiful, nay, sublime exhibitions of the intensity, the depth, the deathlessness of this passion of love. But all we see, all we read of in human history, is but as a ray from the sun, a single drop from the mighty fountain, a ripple on that limitless ocean, which is singled out by Inspiration from other Divine attributes, as the fitting representative of all — the sy̆nonym of Deity.

'God is love.' He so loved the world, that He gave the Son of His bosom to save it from merited destruction. Christ, the Redeemer, loved it even unto death; and he loves it now. And whoever has drunk most deeply of His spirit, shows it most in loving with a Christ-like fervor and self-forgetfulness.

'That the love wherewith Thou hast loved me,' said the Saviour, in that last exquisitely touching, peace-breathing prayer, before the final consummation of His sacrifice,—'That the love wherewith Thou hast loved me, may be in them, and I in them!' What a petition was that, in the illimitable grandeur of its thought, in the rich munificence of its affection. The love wherewith the Father loved His only begotten Son, swelling, surging through the bosom of man, breaking up those deep fountains of the soul, which no mere human finger has the power to reach; and elevating him at once to a new and mysterious connection with the Divine nature! Behold, then, the electric chain that links the family of God on earth; and causes the hearts of all its members to thrill in unison, at the sound of the Controlling Voice! And what says that voice? Appealing in firm, commanding tones, to the principle implanted by the Holy Spirit in the regenerated soul of man, what is its great requirement? GO YE INTO ALL THE WORLD, AND PREACH THE GOSPEL TO EVERY CREATURE!

Is this wise?—is it reasonable?—will it do any good?—inquires the stranger, and while he sits down to doubt and cavil, and search for lions in the way, the unquestioning child goes away and does the Father's bidding. That which is madness and folly in the eyes of one, is regarded by the other as but a simple, affectionate, trustful act of obedience to Him who has the right to control and the power to protect? They have no fears of what the end may be, when He who sees the end from the beginning is directing them. They have not to experiment, and question, and tread doubtfully along the tangled wilderness of life. They have a great unerring Guide, and it is their glory to follow His voice and cling to His hand, through whatever He shall choose to lead them; to believe, to trust, to rejoice in Him, even in the midst of temporary afflictions. And thus it is that they shrink not from the privations, and dangers, and difficulties incident to His service, feeling it their highest honor to be permitted to suffer for His sake. Oh, the love of Christ! the love of Christ! this it is which constitutes the spirit and essence of missionary devotion; and to those who have never drunk from the delicious fountain, who have not yet been made subjects of that wondrous prayer, 'As thou hast loved me,' it may well be looked upon as infatuation.

But 'what has been the fruit of all these labors and sufferings—of all these privations, sacrifices, sicknesses, and deaths?' Nothing to become the ground of boasting, certainly; but enough to make all heaven rejoice. Simply the maturing of a few early clusters of grapes, where only the thorn tree grew; the gathering of a few golden sheaves from the arid soil, which never bore even a blade of grass before. And this is surely worth the labor,. if only as the precursor of a more bountiful harvest. But this is not all that has been done. Behold the rivers of water on their fertilizing course through the desert; look upon the thousand fields laid in long rich furrows by the gospel plough-share, or stirred, and levelled, and wetted with the dews of heaven, waiting for the sower's coming And there are panting hearts, and extended hands, and ready feet, willing, even as the Master wills it, to scatter the seed or gather in the harvest. Ay; go traverse America, from the borders of fair New England to the sounding shores of the Pacific, and count, if they can be counted, the various missionary organizations that have sprung up within the last half century. Go watch the movements of the thousands and tens of thousands of churches by which Christendom is bespangled, and see with what simultaneous action they step forth to the support of the mighty enterprise. Nay, look even at the female sewing-circle, the Sunday School contribution, the infant's penny-box; for know that such are the tiny rills which feed the measureless ocean. Go catch the watchword, 'To every creature! To every creature!' which sounds forth a simultaneous shout, from missionary societies of every evangelical sect; for this one point admits of no jarring or discord.

Go to the records of the Bible Society, and number the tribes and nations, who have already received the word of God in their own tongue. Then turn to these same nations and see them quivering like the leaves of November before the invisible power which is stealing so irresistibly over them. Go, on a holy Sabbath morning, and follow the course of the sun, as he rises on the easternmost port of China, till he climbs over the rocky hills of the far West to garnish the infant spires of Oregon and California. And what changes have not fifty — thirty — ten — nay, five years wrought, throughout that Sabbath track! How the music of the church bells thrills upon the Christian's heart, as on, from port to port, he takes his joyous way! How few and inconsiderable the spots, from which the voice of prayer and praise ascends not, and in which that 'Light of the world,' a Christian church, has not been kindled!

'And what may reasonably be expected to be the fruit?' Ah! that is a theme to stir the golden harps of heaven anew, and make the wide earth vibrate to the joyful harmony. It looks forward to a time when the great family of man shall be united in one holy brotherhood; and there shall be no more war, no more oppression and cruelty, no sinning and no woe. So shall the crimson stain be wiped from the brow of the nations; and the lamb and the dove shall nestle in the shadow of the cross — their peaceful emblems. Then shall the strong protect the weak, and the greatest and most powerful become voluntary servants of the lowly; for the highest type of greatness will be to benefit mankind. This is no poetical illusion — no fair Utopian fancy; nor even a half-formed expectation based on man's weak reason. The believing child knows as certainly as he knows there is a God in heaven, that the mission enterprise cannot fail until it usher in that Sabbath of the world — the Christian Jubilee. And he knows that in that day of Eden purity, and more than Eden elevation, when the lamb and the lion shall lie down together, and HOLINESS shall be inscribed even on the bells of the horses — when the empire of the Son of God shall extend 'from sea to sea, and from the rivers unto the ends of the earth' — there will be in the history of the past no brighter page than the humble tracery of these small beginnings. And when, at last, the heavens are rolled together as a scroll, and the earth disappears from among her sister planets, the fruits of this enterprise shall give richness to the bloom of heaven; and, transmuted to enduring jewels, shall glow with resplendent brilliancy in the crown of man's Redeemer.

SONG OF MAULMAIN.

Ply the lever, pioneers!
Many a waiting angel cheers;
Christ above is interceding,
Here the Holy Ghost is pleading,
  And the promise of Jehovah
    Stands upon His blessed book.
Cheerly, cheerly ply the lever!
Pause not — faint not — falter never!
Course the river, thrid the alley,
From the hill-top to the valley,
  Go this barren border over,
    Scattering seed in every nook.

Gifted with a little wing,
Far the seed shall float and spring, —
Spring and bloom in Burmah's centre,
Till life-giving fragrance enter

Even the sacred groves of Boodha,
And the monarch's golden hall.
Plant the seed, and ply the lever!
Pause not — faint not — falter never!
With a trusting heart and humble,
Toil till Boodha's throne shall crumble,
Monastery and pagoda
Reel before the Cross, and fall.

A LEGEND OF THE MAIZEEN.

'Is he not beautiful, my lord?'

The speaker was a shy, girlish-looking creature, numbering, probably, some sixteen cycles; and, though her cheek and brow had a swarthy hue, and her brilliant black eye glowed with a restless, wild uncertainty of expression, she was yet lavishly gifted with both grace and beauty. She wore over her shoulders a clumsy, bag-like tunic, so profusely ornamented with jungle seeds, glass beads, and the wings of the golden-green beetle, as to conceal the original fabric of blue cotton. Her round, bare arms, were decorated with a variety of fantastic bracelets; and from the knot, into which her shining black hair was gathered, floated the rich golden panicles of the flowery cassia. Her little henna-tipped fingers were busily employed in wreathing chaplets, necklaces, anklets and bracelets, of the rosy white blossoms gathered from a neighboring clerodendron tree, with which she decorated the unshapely person of a tawny infant, sleeping at her knee.

'Is he not beautiful, my lord?' she asked, clapping her hands in childish admiration, after having given to the sylvan costume of her child what she evidently considered the finishing touches.

'My lord'* was a dark, rough, bristly-bearded man, of middle age, unmistakeably Karen in feature, though wearing the Burmese dress, and with it the haughty expression of countenance, characteristic of the latter race. His exterior gave but little promise of sympathy with the flutterings of the young mother's heart, a fact of which she seemed fully aware, for even in her gladness she asked the question with averted

---

*This title is indefinite in the degree of honor which it signifies; being sometimes addressed to royalty, and sometimes conveying so little reverence, as to be better translated *Sir*. It is seldom used by a wife in addressing her husband, unless there is some great difference in rank, or she is kept in unusual subjection.

eye. The appeal, however, was to a father's pride, and he looked at the little brown bundle of flesh, and smiled, at first admiringly, then with a singular expression of contemplative tenderness, of which his stern features were capable, but which they seldom wore.

'What is it?' asked the young wife, apprehensively. 'Is anything the matter with him?'

The father smiled again, a curious smile, mixed up of different expressions, the most prominent of which was a lordly appreciation of his own superior wisdom; while the anxious little mother dropped her flowers upon the bank, and repeated the question,—'Is anything the matter with him?'

'Nothing that you will ever see, my bright little Mango-bird; so keep on singing, while the sun shines.'

'But—but,' she stammered, 'if anything should be the matter with our boy—'

The stern man turned to a clump of thorny bamboos, gracefully mantled by the beautiful Rangoon creeper, and gathering a handful of milk-white blossoms, completed the toilet of the child.

'Beautiful! beautiful!' exclaimed the young mother, quite as much delighted with her husband's condescension, as the effects of his skill.

'Beautiful, and *stainless*, too,' was the response, 'but — ah, you will not understand, my pretty Mimosa; and why should you?'

'I should like to understand, my lord,' and the dark eyes were lifted to his, with a deep, questioning wonder, behind which seemed to lurk some scarcely defined purpose.

The husband, however, remarked nothing unusual.

'Well, Mimosa, you know that when the sun is up, the blossoms will be stained, and so — *our blossom*.'

The woman answered by an absorbed, searching gaze.

'And at evening they will be crimson.'

'*Must* it be so, my lord?'

'Is it not always?'

'What can we do?'

'Nothing.'

The young wife looked disappointed. Several times she opened her lips, as though to speak, but seemed to doubt the wisdom of her purpose; and that strange, fitful light glanced more fitfully than ever from her bright eye. Finally, she leaned over her sleeping child, with a restless sort of anxiety, taking up, one by one, the symbolic blossoms, and breathing on them, while the stern husband stood watching her movements, with an air of amused interest.

'You see that the poison is in you, Mimosa,' he said at length; 'your breath stains the pretty blossoms, and withers them, too,' and he glanced expressively at the child.

The woman made no answer, but she bent still lower, and the struggle, whatever it might be, that was going on in her spirit, seemed almost to convulse her slight frame. The husband regarded her in absolute amazement.

'My poor little Mynah,' he at length said, coaxingly; 'the cage is very dark, but there is no use in beating the bars, and spoiling its pretty wings. Who thought a word would ruffle its plumage so?—there—there!'

The struggle was over; and the woman lifted her head with an air of calm determination.

'My lord, there is at Maulmain city a white foreigner, who teaches that the stain may be removed.'

The dark brows of the husband were suddenly contracted, and a fierce glance shot from his stern eyes; but it was with a quiet, steady voice that he asked, 'Who told you of him, Mynah?'

'My lord!' exclaimed the poor wife, deprecatingly.

'Who told you?' the husband repeated, without elevating his voice, but with a deadly meaning in its cold monotone, which struck a forlorn hopelessness to the heart of that timid young creature, whose very life depended on his nod.

She, however, raised her head with some faint show of courage, and answered, 'I heard it in my father's house, on the other side of the great Salwen.'

'Well, Mimosa, you are not in your father's house now, nor do you tread the white man's territory; and, mark me!' he said, rising and folding his swart arms across his brawny chest, from this moment, you will forget that a word of this abominable heresy has ever entered your ears, or,' with a deeper, sterner intonation, 'that your meddling finger has ever touched their writing. You hear, woman!'

The young wife, like all her race, who have

not been educated out of the national characteristic, was in general docile and submissive; but she evidently had some strong purpose at her heart, a settled determination to bring the subject she had dared present to her husband to some distinct issue. At the last word, fiercely spoken, she sprang to her feet, and confronted the angry man, with her whole frame quivering, and her eye blazing with the intensity of contending emotions.

'What would you do, my lord,' she asked, in a clear, ringing voice, 'if I were to become a Christian?'

'Kill you.'

The woman smiled drearily, sat down, and drew her baby to her bosom.

'Why did you ask such a terrible question, Mimosa?' inquired the husband, after a little pause.

'Because,' she answered, with a short laugh, which might have been simply the overflowing of a careless heart, or, coupled with the words, had something of mockery in it, 'because it is pleasant to know.'

The husband was uncomfortable; perhaps

suspicious. He glanced about him for a new subject, and finally his eye fell upon the round, taper arm, sparkling with most incongruous ornaments. 'What is that odd bracelet, Mimosa, you wear of late?'

'A charm, my lord.'

Something unusual seemed to arrest the woman's attention as she spoke, for she peered for a moment into the forest, then catching up the infant, bounded away.

'Fool! to be frightened by the silly thing,' muttered the husband, following her airy flight with admiring eyes. 'A charm, indeed! That is not like becoming a Christian! Oh, why are there no wise men, no reasoners, no subtle philosophers, among my poor countrymen? Why must they go flocking after every new thing that rises, like silly pigeons to the snare?'

The Karen chief had been educated as a Boodhistic priest, in a Burmese monastery; and had brought to his uncultivated jungle home some of the worst characteristics of the people among whom he had spent his early days. Whatever there might have been kindly in his original disposition, it was completely swept under, by the haughty fierceness in which he now encased himself, as an armor. To those who ministered to his pleasures, and made themselves the slaves of his will, he was sufficiently condescending and indulgent; but woe to that man who dared, even in opinion, to cross his track. He was, also, whether from pride, or religious principle, exceedingly bigoted; and though he could smile, with pitying contempt, on 'charms,' and other superstitions of his degraded countrymen, he could not brook the bare mention of the name of Jesus Christ. Only a little while previous to the commencement of our story, a boat-load of Burmese Christians, who had diverged from the Salwen to the Burmese side, for the purpose of following up the Maizeen rivulet, had been insulted, and ordered away from his village. Still later, a poor Karen, with a bundle of tracts hidden in his rice-basket, had been caught, and severely flogged before the assembled villagers.

It was on the day that the Burman boat had been sent away, that the pretty young wife of the chief wandered down the stream, with an old white-haired man, who had accompanied her from her father's house, and been always in her confidence.

'And you are sure, Pooluah, that my father has embraced this religion?'

'Sure, my lady.'

'And you, Pooluah?'

The old man hesitated. He was something of a courtier; but that might not have been his only reason for answering, 'It is better that my lady examine for herself. Old Pooluah is *her* follower.'

'Was that the reason you taught me to read Burmese—that I might examine for myself? Did you think of it then, when I used to lead you such a wild race through the paddy-fields? Ah, Pooluah, he calls me, when he is fondest, his mynah, and it is true. I am a poor caged mynah now, and shall never fly again.'

The old man sighed; and they both relapsed into sad, musing silence.

'My lady,' said Pooluah, at length, peering down the river, 'what is that, yonder, like a little foam-curl on the water, there by the roots of the nodding clerodendron?'

'A cluster of blossoms, I think; or it may

be——' and without waiting for further speculation, she tripped away to the spot indicated. Poising herself on the twisted roots of the clerodendron, she grasped a branch with one hand, and leaning far over, she was just able to secure with the other the object of the old man's curiosity.

'A writing! a writing!' she shouted, forgetting all caution in her sudden delight, and flourishing her prize aloft. But, at that moment, her foot slipped; the bough by which she steadied herself, swept across her face, she felt herself seized and dragged upon the bank by a stronger arm than that of her age-enfeebled attendant, and saw, as she opened her eyes, the frowning face of her husband bending over her.

'Did you mean to drown yourself, Mimosa?' he asked, in a tone of suppressed anger.

'I might possibly have bathed my foot,' the woman answered, with affected carelessness, though visibly shuddering as she spoke. She had been fully aware, even in the confusion occasioned by her slight accident, that there was more of fierceness and roughness in her husband's mode of saving her, than the danger seemed to warrant; and she was, moreover, conscious of the writing's having been wrenched from her hand and flung into the rivulet.

The husband and wife walked back to the village together. A couple of fishermen had just moved their little boat beside the clump of bamboos, and the chief beckoned one of them with his hand.

'Ho, Pantalay!'

The man came forward, crouching with the customary reverence, and squatted respectfully at the chieftain's feet.

'What was that you were telling me, yesterday, of the golden book?'

'My lord!' exclaimed the poor man, with a look of terror.

The chief made an impatient gesture; but the man's stupidity was incorrigible.

'My lord commanded — he — he said the tale was false and idle.'

The Mimosa smiled involuntarily; and the angry chief raised his hand as though to strike the stammering offender. He did not strike, however, but only reiterated, 'What was it, Pantalay?'

The poor fellow began deprecatingly to repeat the tale which only the day before he had been ordered never to think of again. The substance of it was that a boatman from the lower province of Tavoy had reported the arrival of a white teacher there, who, by the help of a Karen man he had bewitched, was scattering strange writings through the jungle. He also averred that a golden book had fallen down from heaven, threatening the direst vengeance on all who presumed to read, or even touch these writings.

'What vengeance, Pantalay?'

'They — they shall be haunted by demons, while they sleep and when they wake. The women shall be childless, or bear monsters, and the men shall be devoured by tigers on the land, and by alligators on the water.'

'That will do, Pantalay.'

The chief evidently felt that there had been a failure in the poor fisherman's mode of telling the tale; but still it was not without its effect on the timid Mimosa.

A few days after this event, the poor Karen book-bearer was apprehended and whipped; and then crawled away into the jungle, some said, to die. Only old Pooluah, and his gentle-hearted mistress, knew of a small cave among the craggy heights beyond the village, where the poor fellow was nursed until his wounds were healed, and he was able to make his escape over to the English side of the Salwen. Even the Mimosa herself had found means to visit him, and he had told her all he knew of the Christian religion. His knowledge was very limited indeed; but in nothing is the loving kindness of our Heavenly Father more beautifully displayed, than in the simplicity of the doctrines which lead to salvation. A theme which the angels around the blazing throne have not yet fully comprehended, is so completely adapted to our human wants, that the weakest capacity — nay, even the lowest, and most animalized nature, needs but the influences of the Holy Spirit to be able to put forth a saving faith. Old Pooluah drank in the truth with a simple earnestness, for which he was already prepared by the visit of the Christian boatmen, as well as by hints and rumors he had occasionally heard before he followed his mistress from her old home. The Mimosa, with stronger worldly interests, was less trustful and more cautious. She looked at her child, and thought of the golden book with its terrible maledictions; and, though she had sufficient shrewdness to understand her husband's object, in having it related just at that time, she still felt strongly impressed by it. From the date of the visit of the Burmese boat, which her husband had ordered so peremptorily from the village, a thoughtful seriousness had gradually infused itself into her spirit, and it was deepened by every interview with old Pooluah, and still more with the poor Karen fugitive. A little tract, an epitomized 'View of the Christian Religion,' written in Burmese, had been conveyed to her in a basket of flowers, only an hour before the flogging had taken place; and this she had carefully folded together in a deer-skin case, elaborately ornamented with wild seeds, and bound it on her arm with her other bracelets. It was the safest place in which such a treasure could be hidden, and would be always at hand for perusal. This was the odd bracelet, that, at such an inopportune moment, had attracted the attention of her husband.

'A charm,' she answered, unhesitatingly, to his abrupt question; then, terrified at her danger, ashamed of her weakness, and conscious of being unable to sustain farther scrutiny, she snatched up the child, and hastened away. Rapidly she sped along, not venturing to look behind to ascertain whether she was pursued, now pressing through thick underbrush, now mounting some flower-mantled hillock, and again plashing across the pretty silver runnels that laced the wilderness, till she had left a quarter of a league behind her. She was still hurrying on, when a familiar voice exclaimed, in some surprise, 'My lady!' It was old Pooluah, who was returning from a foraging expedition, his withered frame more than usually bowed beneath the heavy bundle of fresh herbs he had just been gathering.

'Has anything happened, my lady?'

'Happened! no; but there will—there *must*, and I almost wish it would come now.'

'Look to the Lord Jesus Christ, my lady. He

is strong. He never deserts them who put their trust in Him.'

'I do not put my trust in Him, Pooluah. I am not a Christian. When you are in trouble, you can pray like the poor book-bearer, and your mind becomes cool and happy. I cannot. I do not trust Him. I shrink, I tremble, and dare not even tell the truth.'

'My lady —'

'I said just now, Pooluah, that it was a *charm* I wore upon my arm. I told a falsehood, and all from fear. I am a poor, timid woman, and I can *never* be a Christian.'

'My dear lady, you are sorely tempted. But try — try, my sweet mistress, to bring your trouble to the Lord. He will take it willingly. He has trodden all these dark ways, and he knows every step. Cannot you trust Him, my lady?'

The woman shook her head. 'I am a poor, caged mynah, and must obey my keeper. I thought his mind was softened, Pooluah, for he talked of our common sin, as though sorry for it; so I ventured to tell him there was a way of escape, and he was — oh, *so* angry! If it had been red anger, I might have braved it, but it was the white heat, that emits no sparkles. He says he will kill me, if I become a Christian. I am young to die — and the grave is so dark — and I cannot take my little white-souled blossom with me, *if* I could! I am young to die, Pooluah.' And the poor, helpless creature threw herself upon the sod, and wept passionately. The old man lowered the bundle of herbs from his head, slid the heavy satchel from his shoulder, and sat down beside her.

'Old Pooluah's sun is almost down, my lady, and his life is worth but little. Would that it were fresh and bright, as in other days, and he might be permitted to give it in exchange for thine.'

'I know you love me, my faithful Pooluah; but you are all.'

'The Lord Jesus Christ loves you, my lady.'

'I cannot feel it — I dare not think of it. The way is dark, dark.'

'He gave His royal limbs to the torture, and His body to the tomb, for you, my lady. It *is* dark, the world is *all* dark; but He came down from glory, and waded through the darkness and the sorrow, for you, my dear lady, for you. You think old Pooluah is faithful, because he would not keep back this little fragment of a worn-out life from his mistress' service — the Lord gave all, and He is all-powerful. Trust in Him, my lady — lay your little white-souled blossom on His bosom — lay your sorrows at His feet — and the shadow of Death itself will never make you afraid.'

Thus, in a low, tender tone, as a mother might soothe her frightened infant, the old man's words mingled with the passionate sobbings of the young matron, and settled, like a healing balsam, on her heart.

'But I denied Him, Pooluah; and denied Him insultingly. I said it was a charm I wore —'

'It was in a moment of weakness, my lady; you were sorely tempted. Call upon the Lord. He is a pitying Redeemer. Ask Him to forgive you, to strengthen you, to support you in the hour of trial, and when the way is all dark, look to Him, my lady, and light will come.'

From the day of this conversation, a change began to be perceptible in the once timid

Mimosa, which gradually pervaded her entire character. She seemed, by degrees, endowed with a sublime courage, a spirit like that of the martyrs of old, sufficient to buoy her above all fear. This was too apparent in the serene, elevated expression of her countenance, and her general bearing, to escape the observation of the villagers; who whispered to one another that she had probably received some intelligence from her father, which enabled her to brave her husband's more than suspected tyranny. But the real cause of the transformation was not long hidden. Ashamed of the falsehood, which she interpreted into a denial of her faith, the repentant young believer unbound the bracelet from her arm, threw the deer-skin case into the river, and sought no other concealment for the book than one of the hollow bamboo rafters of her dwelling — so easy of access, and in such common use, as to be a mere depository, rather than a hiding-place. But this was not all. Defying all the cautions of the faithful Pooluah, she began whispering the glad news of salvation among the villagers; and so much was she beloved, and the fearful vengeance of her husband so much dreaded, that even the most uncompromising Boodhists failed to betray her. So month after month passed by, and seasons came and went. There were no withering leaves or falling snows — our way-marks through the year — but yet the circling seasons left their footprints on the tropic jungle, scarcely less strongly marked than on our rugged shores.

The amber sunlight of a rich October day was deepening into purple, when the young jungle matron sat watching the gambols of her boy, and musing on the prospect of yet another little being, which might ere long be intrusted to her care to train for immortality. Her piety had deepened very perceptibly during the passing year, and a meek, trustful wisdom had gradually infused itself into her spirit, softening and ripening her whole character. The little book was now so much worn by frequent use, as to be in many places illegible; but the truths it contained were perfectly familiar to the young matron, though still she loved to read them from the page where they had first met her eye and heart. With this object, she took the book from a little pocket she had made for it in her tunic, and was soon absorbed in its contents. She was roused by a rough grasp on her shoulder, and a voice in stern, angry accents, exclaiming, 'Woman! woman! what have you here?' For a moment her brain reeled, and her heart grew faint; for though she had expected an hour like this to come, it had been so long delayed, that she had ceased to look for it momentarily, as at first. She, however, retained sufficient composure of manner to answer, though somewhat tremulously, 'It is a — a foreign book, my lord.'

'One of those vile books ——'

'It is not a vile book,' interrupted the woman, dauntlessly.

'Which — which I commanded you not to touch!'

'Should I not obey God rather than ——'

'Silence, babbler! slave!' — Then smothering his rage again, 'But where is the traitor that dared to give you this?'

'I had it, my lord, of the poor fellow, who a year ago was whipped for having Christian books in his rice-basket.'

'And you have kept it ever since?'

'I have, my lord.'

'And read it?'

'I have.'

He snatched the book from her hand, and tore it into fragments.

'That is useless, my lord. It matters little to destroy the paper, when every word is cut into my memory.'

'You will not say that you believe that book?'

'I do.'

'And you dare tell me this!—that you are an idiot—a mountebank—a—a—'

'I am a Christian, my lord.'

The stern man shook with concentrated passion; but still he so far mastered it, as to proceed with his examination.

'Who knows you are—what you say?'

The woman was silent.

'Speak! I command you.'

'I cannot tell, my lord.'

'What! you—you—you—defy me?'

'I will answer all questions that concern myself, my lord, but farther than that, I cannot.'

'You refuse, then, to mention your accomplices.'

'I refuse to betray my friends.'

The brawny arm seemed to leap into the air, with the quick violence of overwhelming rage, and the next moment the courageous young wife lay writhing upon the earth, a crimson stream gushing from her distended mouth. With a wild, unearthly cry, which drew a dozen villagers to the spot, the strange man threw himself beside his victim, his fierce anger in a moment yielding to the still more terrific fury of his grief.

'I have killed her! I have killed her! her — my golden lily — my bundle of musk! I have darkened my eyes! I have torn the heart from my bosom! I am a murderer, sinking down — down — down to the lowest hell. Oh, Mimosa! my beautiful, pitying Mimosa! do not begin the torments now, while yet thy lip is warm with life. Speak to me! oh speak, Mimosa! I meant not to strike. It was the demon in me, and not my hand. One little word — one breath — my beautiful, my loved, my lost Mimosa!' And while, with all the energy of that one anguish-stricken voice, the death-wail rang through the jungle, the villagers, awed and terrified, dared not so much as lay a finger upon the murdered woman. Old Pooluah was the last to reach the spot. With one deep, heart-crushing inspiration, he sprang forward, and taking his mistress in his arms, bore her to the shelter of her own home.

For hours there was a faint fluttering of the pulse, and an occasional tremulous motion of the eyelids; but that was all. Old Pooluah watched beside his mistress, and two or three women moved noiselessly about the room; but the husband came not, all through the dreary night. At last, when the first ray of morning shot through the open door, the dying Mimosa opened wide her joyous eyes.

'Pooluah!' she called.

The old man stooped above her.

'Dear, faithful Pooluah, take the little boy to my father, and tell him — oh, tell him how sweet it is to die. Though so young, and so unworthy, I am permitted first to enter the celestial gate, and there I wait both you and him. How beautiful! how glorious!'

With that rejoicing smile upon her lip, the

young Christian passed away — slept in Jesus; and another life slept with her.

The stern chief never returned to his village, and his fate was never clearly known. Some told how, on the night of the direful tragedy, a party of boatmen near the mouth of the Maizeen, had seen a crouching figure pass fleetly as a shadow, just outside their circle of camp-fires. They hailed him, but received no answer. A quarter of an hour afterwards, a wild, terrible cry of mortal agony rang from the jungle, and with trembling hands the men brightened their watch-fires, and grasped their spears, and so sat with unclosed eyes till morning. As the dawn advanced, the little party gathered more courage; and finally, fully armed, ventured forward in the direction of the cry. Parting the thick boughs, not more than a hundred rods from where they had encamped, they found the underbrush crushed and trampled, and the sod besmeared with gore. A small crimson pool had settled down into a leafy hollow, and a muslin turban, torn and blood-stained, lay at a little distance on the ground. Remembering that the tiger which has once tasted human blood is never satisfied with a single victim, the men returned hastily to their boat. The more sanguinary of the villagers, as they told this story, were wont to illustrate its meaning and application with expressive glances and gestures, though they never by words indicated any positive suspicion as to the victim.

Then some gentle spirit would take up the tale, and describe a bent, hollow-eyed, witless man, who haunted the suburbs and lanes of Martaban, muttering to himself continually, and appearing startled when overheard, as though he had betrayed some secret. It was remarked that he dwelt with strange pertinacity on one word, which might be a name, since he whispered it so beseechingly, by the hour together; but those persons who were curious enough to listen, were surprised to learn that he only addressed a pretty plant, such as is often found in the neighborhood of deserted monasteries, and the leaves of which are wont to shrivel and fall to the ground at the slightest touch. Then the narrator would look into the incredulous faces of the propagators of the tiger-tale, and nod his head significantly, and say what an odd fancy it was that the chief should have named his pretty wife *Mimosa*.

Sometimes a singular story of a sound man herding with lepers, and voluntarily performing the most menial offices of the community, was darkly hinted at. And there was yet another tale afloat, of a hermit-priest, who inhabited the beautiful little gem of an island in the Salwen, known as Goungzakyoon. But the narratives relating to this last named personage were of a shifting, mythic order; and as they were put forth by the more bigoted of the Boodhistic party, they obtained but little credence from the greater number of the Karens.

NOTE. — The recorder of the above legend does not vouch for its accuracy; none of the particulars having come under the personal observation of the friend from whom she received it. As a story quite current among the early Karen Christians, however, and neither unnatural nor improbable in its general features, (though the principal characters are certainly more Burmese than Karen,) it bears the stamp of truth. The writer, in giving the relation an English dress, has taken the liberty to divest it of some of the childish mysteries which cluster around it, and to reduce it, as far as possible, to the order of a simple narrative.

THE JUNGLE BOY.

Many years ago, a lady sat in the verandah of her Burmese bungalow, endeavoring to decipher the scarcely legible characters of a palm-leaf book, which lay in all its awkwardness upon the table before her. A beautiful beetle, with just gold enough on his bright green wings to distinguish him from the glossy leaves of the Cape Jasmine, which grew close by the balustrade, was balancing himself upon one of the rich white blossoms that filled the whole air with their fragrance; while a gay-plumaged bird, with a strange sort of a feathery coronal upon his head, was making himself busy among the rank grass beyond. Still farther on, a long-necked chamelion clung to the trunk of a guava tree, throwing back his snake-like head, and darting his inquisitive little eyes about very suspiciously; a green-coated robber of a parrot nestled among the fruit and foliage above; and below, and all around, a whole school of crows flapped their black wings, and wheeled, and fluttered, and cawed, with amazing industry and volubility. It is in vain to try to enumerate the lady's strange visitors, but they were such as any of you might see of a bright morning in Burmah, and very attractive you would find them — much more attractive, I have no doubt, than the long palm-leaf books, all smeared with oil, to make their circular scratches legible. From a little bamboo shelter — a curious thatched roof set upon poles, just beyond the high, uncropped hedge, and dignified by the name of schoolhouse — came a sound of mingled voices, very cheerful, very earnest, and, to stranger ears, about as intelligible as the cawing of the crows. But the lady understood it all; and it told her that her native schoolmaster was doing his duty, and his tawny pupils making some proficiency in the *them-bōng gyee*, or a-b, ab talk. *Kah gyee yă, ka — kah gyee yă kya, käh — kah gyee yă lōng gyee ten, kĕ — kah gyee yă lōng gyee ten san cat, kēe*, came the confused sounds — a very circuitous way of saying k-a, ka — k-e, ke, — 'Don't you think so?'

As the lady bent over her book, a little more wearily than in the freshness of the morning, and made a renewed effort to fix her eyes on the dizzying circles, a strange looking figure bounded through the opening in the hedge which served as a gateway, and rushing toward her, with great eagerness inquired, 'Does Jesus Christ live here?'

He was a boy, perhaps twelve years of age; his coarse black hair unconfined by the usual turban, matted with filth, and bristling in every direction like the quills of a porcupine; and a very dirty cloth of plaided cotton disposed in the most slovenly manner about his person.

'Does Jesus Christ live here?' he inquired, scarcely pausing for breath, though slackening his pace a little as he made his way, uninvited, up the steps of the verandah, and crouched at the lady's feet.

'What do you want of Jesus Christ?' inquired the lady.

'I want to see him — I want to confess to him.'

'Why, what have you been doing, that you want to confess?'

'*Does he live here?*'—with great emphasis,—'I want to know *that*. Doing! Why, I tell lies, I steal, I do everything bad—I am afraid of going to hell, and I want to see Jesus Christ, for I heard one of the *Loo-gyees** say that he can save us from hell. Does he live here? Oh, tell me where I can find Jesus Christ.'

'But he does not save people from hell, if they continue to do wickedly.'

'I want to stop doing wickedly, but I can't stop—I don't know how to stop—the evil thoughts are in me, and the bad deeds come of evil thoughts. What can I do?'

'Nothing, but come to Christ, poor boy, like all the rest of us,' the lady softly murmured; but she spoke this last in English, so the boy only raised his head with a vacant,—'B' ha-lai?'

'You cannot see Jesus Christ now—'

She was interrupted by a sharp quick cry of despair.

---

* Chief men.

'But I am his humble friend and follower'— The face of the listener brightened a little.

'And he has commissioned me to teach all those who wish to escape from hell, how to do so.'

The joyful eagerness depicted in the poor boy's countenance, was beyond description. 'Tell me—oh tell me! Only ask your Master the Lord Jesus Christ, to save me, and I will be your servant, your slave, for life. Do not be angry! Do not send me away! I want to be saved—saved from hell!'

The lady, you will readily believe, was not likely to be angry. Even the person who told me the story many years after, was more than once interrupted by his own choking tears.

The next day a new pupil was welcomed to the little bamboo schoolhouse, in the person of the wild Karen boy; for no missionary having yet been sent especially to that people, they received all their religious instructions through the medium of the Burmese language. And oh, *such* a greedy seeker after truth and holiness! Every day he came to the white teachers to learn something more concerning the Lord Jesus

Christ, and the way of salvation; and every day his mind seemed to open, his feelings to enlarge, and his face to lose some portion of that indescribable look of stupidity which characterizes the uncultivated native.

In due time, a sober band of worshippers gathered around the pool in the little hollow by the bridge, to witness a solemn baptism; then a new face was seen among those who came to commemorate the dying love of the Lord Jesus; and a new name was written on the church records.

Years passed away. Death had laid his hand upon the gentle lady, and she had gone up to that sweet home where pain and sorrow are unknown, and where 'the weary are at rest.' On earth, another death scene was enacting. A strong, dark-browed man tossed wildly on his fevered couch in an agony of physical suffering; but even then his unconscious lips murmured continually those precious fragments of scripture which he had treasured up in days of health. At last there came a fearful struggle — then the convulsed features relaxed, the ghastliness of death settled upon them, and the spirit seemed to have taken its flight. Suddenly, however, the countenance of the dying man was lighted with a heavenly radiance, his lips parted with a smile, his eye emitted a single joyful flash, before it turned cold and motionless forever; and then the wild boy of the jungle was welcomed by his waiting angel-guide, to the presence of that Saviour whom he had sought with such eagerness.

TRIBUTE TO REV. DANIEL HASCALL.

Lo! with a solemn tread,
The mourning train sweep by,
Bearing the sainted dead,
To where his loved ones lie;
Down in his bed of clay,
They lay him to his rest,
The sun-light shut away,
And the clod upon his breast.

Will they the marble bring? —
Nay, look around and see
How many a nobler thing
His monument shall be.
Behold yon classic walls,*
Embalmed in love and prayer,
Pause in the shadowy halls, —
His monument is there!

---

* In the year 1817, Mr. Hascall commenced a theological school in the village of Hamilton, N. Y., with the two mis-

And with enduring art,
  Is sculptured his fair fame,
Upon each living heart,
  That thrills beneath his name.
Where waves the tropic palm,
  Where ice-bound fir-trees grow,
'Mid island groves of balm,
  'Mid northern wilds of snow,

Tho' his name be never heard,
  The deeds of love he 's wrought,
Are told in every word,
  Are mirrored in each thought;
While angels stooping down,
  On fondly fluttering wing,
Pluck jewels for the crown
  Of our Eternal King.

Those jewels saved in heaven,
  And the garnered prayers and tears,
All good for which he 's striven,
  Through weary, toilsome years;

---

sionaries, Wade and Kincaid, for his first pupils. The school, which has now grown into a University, has, probably, contributed as large a number of devoted and practical men to the mission enterprise, as any similar institution in America.

Up in that world of rest,
  His monument shall be;
For the spring his finger pressed,
  Has moved eternity.

THE MOST EFFICIENT MISSIONARIES.

AMONG the various opinions which prevail with regard to the qualifications most desirable in a missionary, care must be taken that the building and garnishing do not occupy too prominent a position, to the detriment of the richer inheritance of the spirit. Devotion to Christ and love to man are, after all, the great qualifications.

Some seven or eight years ago, there came to Maulmain a fine old British officer, who had in the dawn of his career served in the Peninsular wars, and brought away a French love-token, in the shape of an honorable scar, from the battle of Salamanca. He was an earnest, active, fearless sort of a man, and yet not particularly gifted with anything, except the life-giving influences of the Holy Spirit. In his regiment he was a sort of dissenting chaplain ; in the little English church he was the first in every good word and work ; and in the prison and hospital he was like a ministering angel, until forbidden by his superior to degrade his office by familiar intercourse with the common soldier; and then he submissively took his stand in the doorway, and read and preached the gospel to the sick and the friendless within. Thus much for his own countrymen — but that was not all. His association with the American missionaries opened a new field of usefulness, and in spite of jeers, reproaches and expostulations, he entered upon it manfully. By the help of a Burmese Christian, who had been taught the English, he went up street and down, preaching the gospel to all he met, and distributing tracts from the ample satchel of his interpreter. He also stood in the zayat by the wayside, assailing every passer-by; he entered the lowly doors of the lowliest natives; and in the monasteries he boldly opposed his own commission to the lofty pretensions of the proud proprietors of the shaven crown and yellow robe.

Now that is the sort of man, whatever his

other qualifications may be, most needed in the great missionary work. The command of the Lord Jesus Christ, 'Go ye into all the world, and preach the gospel to every creature,' was not addressed to ministers alone, and is no more restricted to a particular style of man, or a particular set of qualifications, than it was to the twelve disciples. The commission includes every man, woman and child who loves the Saviour. It is addressed personally and distinctly to each one; and whoever evades it in this enlightened age, should at least be prepared with reasons to present at the bar of God. Every converted soul has a duty to perform to his fellow-men. If he cannot GO — if he is sure, positively sure, that he has an excuse which will stand the searching light of eternity, let him stay at home, and help others go. But if he has not that excuse, he is disobeying the last positive command of his ascending Lord. And though, through the sufferings of that slighted Saviour, he may be so forgiven as not to prove an outcast from the realms of bliss, just so sure as 'one star differeth from another star in glory,' will he be crippled for his remissness, throughout the never-ending ages of eternity. I am advocating no wild theory; I speak the words of truth and soberness. And in doing so, I appeal to conscious hearts. Are there not hundreds — aye, thousands of truly converted men in our American churches, — who dare not — *dare not* enter the closet, and there, making an unreserved consecration of self, solemnly pray for light on the subject of personal duty? No; I will make no such general appeal; but *you* — you who hold this paper — dare *you* do it? Have you ever done it? Will you do it now, or do you fear the result?

'I have an extensive business.'

Ah! 'I have bought five yoke of oxen.' That is it.

'I have a family.'

'He that loveth son or daughter —' Take care!

'I am approaching middle age.'

And therefore should make the greater haste, remembering at the same time, for your encouragement, that 'they received every man a penny.'

'I believe the conversion of the world is to

be a gradual thing.' It is to be feared that it will, until persecution scatters the church, which is hedging herself round with worldly comforts, and forgetting the noble purpose for which she was raised up. And there are things in the political and religious horizon, which foretell a day of persecution, now not far distant.

But I am wandering from my subject. While the great mass of Christians are waiting to be *driven out*, while one only in thousands will go or can be sent, should not that one be of the very choicest kind? Yes, as has been often said, the church must yield up her jewels, her richest and her brightest. But what is it that constitutes the brightness of the Christian jewel? What was it that made the face of Moses to shine, when he came forth from communion with God? Yes, let the church give her best men — men of the warmest hearts, the strongest faith, the most prayerful spirits — men, who think meanly of themselves, and feel that they are honored in being permitted to engage in this Christ-like work — and not that their poor weak intellects, and paltry accomplishments, confer honor on the cause. That is what is holding back the chariot-wheels of God. Wise men think they stoop, they condescend, when they become missionaries. Well, let the wise men — the Pharisees and Sadducees — go their ways. Take the humble, zealous, faithful fishermen of Galilee, and God will use the weak things of this world to confound the mighty. Men, whose hearts are overflowing with the love of Christ, in whatever walks of life they may be found, will always make the most efficient missionaries.

MISAPPREHENSION.

By the September number of the Macedonian, I perceive that some loose remarks of mine in a former number, have had the misfortune to be entirely misunderstood; and that, too, by an old friend, and once spiritual instructor. In the article entitled 'The most Efficient Missionaries,' there was certainly no intended disparagement of talent and learning. But, as these constitute a species of riches in little danger of being undervalued at the present age, and fully able to vindicate their own claim to honor and preferment; while calling attention to matters of higher importance, it seemed perfectly safe to leave this point to its own natural guards. The writer of 'Missionary Qualifications,' however, viewing the subject from a different side, seems to regard the omission as a declaration of mischievous sentiments; and so has taken a more antagonistic position probably than he is aware of. His article appears based on the supposition (*appears* only, for he surely cannot mean it), that Christianity is equally honored by all who actually possess it; or, in other words, that there are no higher spiritual attainments, than those which are 'indispensable to every Christian character.' 'In enumerating,' says he, 'the qualifications of a man for manual labor, it is needless to state that he has a *hand*.' True, but is it not very important to know what that hand may be in the way of muscular power and general adaptedness to the proposed object? 'In speaking,' he continues, 'of the fitness of one for mental labor, it is unnecessary to premise that he has a *mind*.' Is it not a question of some moment, however, what sort of mind he has? 'And,' he concludes, 'in speaking of the qualifications of a Christian missionary, it need not be said he is a *Christian*. That is taken for granted,' &c. And is that really enough? After the granted fact, that a Christian missionary is a Christian, do his mental powers come next in review? So should not one of the most devoted of modern missionaries even *seem* to teach. As though there were no grades of spiritual life! as though it were a matter of little or no importance that they who stand nearest the Master, and enter most deeply into His counsels should proclaim His will; or as though the work might be trusted with equal confidence to the half-hearted disciple, who follows afar off, and has his vision dimmed and his hearing dulled by the thousand earthly shapes and sounds that intervene!

After admitting the gospel messenger to the matter-of-course community of 'love to God and love to man,' what are 'the gifts and graces peculiar to the ministry?' Surely not those mental powers shared by the instructor, the physician, and the lawyer. Oh, no! Infinitely beyond these are the higher gifts and graces of the Spirit — not *peculiar* indeed to any profession, because attainable by every child of God, but preëminently *the* qualifications essential to the minister and the missionary. Oh, it is not true, it cannot be true, that the grand intellectual 'lion' is of more use in the vineyard of the Lord, than the faithful 'dog,' watching his Master's eye, and obeying the slightest indication of His will. True, the lion may be used upon occasion, because the Hand that made has power to tame him; and so effectually may he be tamed, as to stand forth a most beautiful and symmetrical exhibition of the power of Divine Grace. We have had such lions in our own age, raised up for special purposes; and in the apostolic age, Paul was one; and farther back, passing by many others, stands Moses. But the real power of these wonderful men (giving full credit to their intellectual greatness) was not an original inheritance, nor the superadded culture and accomplishments incident to their position. By faith, Moses wrought; and by the inspiration of God, Paul reasoned.

The allusion to the apostle James at Jerusalem, starts quite another topic. Were the question asked me, which stand most in need of a high order of talent, severe mental discipline, and varied attainments, the pastors of Boston, New York, and Philadelphia, or the missionaries of China, Burmah, and other eastern lands, — I should have no hesitation in saying, *the latter, by a hundred-fold.* The one wields a limited, however important influence in a polished community; the other, under God, sways the destinies of a nation. The one needs skill in using the instruments furnished to his hand; the other must have the science to investigate, and the genius to create. England develops her strongest, her most powerful minds, in the rich soil of the Orient; and there, too, must the American churches look for their great men — men who, in accordance with the Saviour's type of greatness, have become voluntary servants of their brethren. This position might be proved by argument and by illustration. It might be shown how, in sending out different kinds of material, the lead had become silver, and the brass gold; and how the gold had been refined and polished till men were astonished at its brightness; but offering a premium to ambition might prove a yet more dangerous experiment than the deprecated 'premium to ignorance.'

So, since it seems necessary to define one's position accurately, the 'objections' of the writer 'to ministerial education and missionary qualifications,' stand something on this wise. God has made it our duty to cultivate the minds he has given us to the extent of their capacities, so far as we have means and opportunity; and ignorance, at the present day, except under peculiar and uncontrollable circumstances, is a sin. Let our spiritual teachers, both at home and abroad, be men of disciplined minds and habits, endowed with intellectual graces and manly accomplishments to the full; but let them know and feel that, after all, these are, in the great work of the Lord, only secondary qualifications. The strong, throbbing pulse of spiritual life; the meek, self-denying soul, attuned to the harmonious breathings of the great Comforter; the 'lips touched with a live coal from the altar' of God; and the heart so Christ-like in its great, wide-spreading love, as to thrill beneath every touch of human sympathy—these are the 'gifts and graces' without which even a Paul would labor in vain. These are things not depending on human wisdom, and as far above it as the Word of God is above all human books; and these, I repeat, in whatever walks of life they may be found, will ever constitute the most efficient missionary.

THE WAN REAPERS.

I CAME from a land where a beautiful light
  Is slow creeping o'er hill-top and vale;
Where broad is the field, and the harvest is
    white,
  But the reapers are haggard and pale.

All wasted and worn with their wearisome toil,
  Still they pause not—that brave little band;
Though soon their low pillows must be the
    strange soil
  Of that distant and grave-dotted strand.

For dangers uncounted are clustering there,—
  The pestilence stalks uncontrolled;
Strange poisons are borne on the soft, languid
    air,
  And lurk in each leaf's fragrant fold.

There the rose never blooms on fair woman's
    wan cheek,

But there 's beautiful light in her eye;
And the smile that she wears is so loving and meek,
None can doubt it comes down from the sky.

There the strong man is bowed in his youth's golden prime,
But he cheerily sings at his toil,
For he thinks of his sheaves and the garnering time
Of the glorious Lord of the soil.

And ever they turn — that brave, wan, little band —
A long, wistful gaze on the West: —
'Do they come — do they come from that dear, distant land,
That land of the lovely and blest?

'Do they come — do they come? — Oh, we're feeble and wan,
And we're passing like shadows away;
But the harvest is white, — and lo! yonder the dawn!
For laborers — for laborers we pray!'

THE HEATHEN BETTER THAN CHRISTIANS.

'It is not to be denied, that people are worse in Christendom than in heathen lands. My own belief is, that there is more evil of a soul-destroying character committed in London in one year, than in Hindostan in ten years; and that London, Paris, and New York stand more in need of missionaries than all heathendom.

'If they' [Messrs. Judson and Parker] 'were to spend as much time in some parts of Christendom, as they have spent in heathen lands, I doubt not that they would agree with me, that "Charity begins at home."

'Paul says, "For when the Gentiles, which have not the law, do by nature the things contained in the law, those having not the law, are a law unto themselves;" and throughout the whole chapter where he thus speaks, clearly shows that if the Gentiles do what is right according to this law written upon their hearts, they will be accepted.' — *Correspondent of the Columbian Magazine.*

THIS is certainly an age of wonderful discoveries — discoveries in ethics, as well as in physics; but it has been reserved for the 'Prince of moralists' to make the most astounding revelation of all — to announce to a Christian community, that Christianity is actually demoralizing. True, there have been open, every-day practices in Hindostan, that would make the vilest wretches who congregate in St. Giles or at the Five Points, turn pale with horror; but then, the sin was not of 'a soul-destroying character,' for these happy heathen were 'a law unto themselves,' until English law and Christian missionaries cast a blight upon their pristine purity, and converted into crime such petty pastimes as drowning an infant, burning a widow, or training a whole caste to the pious trade of assassinating the lonely traveller.

The sea-weary voyager, entering the Bay of Bengal, will no doubt look upon the group of beautiful islands, which sit upon the waters, wrapped in their mantle of soft, purple light, as an oriental Eden; and they are, indeed, not only peculiarly oriental, but one of those Edens where men are 'a law unto themselves.' If a vessel be stranded on their coast, the affrighted crew will commit themselves to the wildest hurricane seaward, in preference to the tender mercies of paradisiacal arrows and cooking-pots. It has been confidently asserted that the delicate stomachs of this primitive race of men, turn in disgust from all inferior viands, to dine with peculiar zest off a barbecued European; but as no man has ever returned to tell the tale of his having been eaten, the gentle Andamaners are certainly entitled to the benefit of a doubt. I think, however, that no missionary will rashly covet the distinction of putting the matter to the test; and so philanthropists of a certain school may have the pleasure of knowing that the vices of Christianity will probably be slow in reaching the Andamans. Then there are the Khonds — what a charming people they are, to be sure, with their primitive, unsophisticated ways! And what a pity that narrow-minded, meddling Christians should interfere with such beautiful arrangements as penning up bands of boys and girls, to be fattened and scientifically sliced, that their yet palpitating flesh and bubbling blood may manure the soil of their native plains. What a pity that the missionaries, who are now feeding, clothing, and instructing the five hundred and forty youths rescued from a doom so exceedingly primeval in its Cain-like simplicity, had not remained in London, making money for their own children, and training them up to imitate parental selfishness — to believe that 'Charity begins at home,' *and ends there!* And what a pity that any lady, occupying the social position of the two who serve to point the moral of our author's tale — a lady who, as everybody knows, can find abundance of time to dress, shop, visit, embroider pretty ottomans, read pleasing stories, and do whatever else fancy may dictate — what a pity that she, with her half dozen children, actually revelling in the rich blessings of a Christian home, should occasionally spare an hour to a missionary magazine, and a dollar to the mission treasury, in behalf of the orphaned, the desolate, and degraded of another land!

Absurd as the broad assertion of our moralist may appear to those who have been favored with a wider field of observation, it is only the caricature of a sentiment in which a certain class of philanthropists seem to take especial delight. In proof of this, one need but glance at the pretty pictures of American savages and dark-eyed orientals, which figure so largely in poetry and romance; and which are about as true to the original, as would be a mortal's map of fairy-land. And if the missionary's daring pencil venture upon a few of the black shadows, which in truth constitute nine tenths of the real landscape, — why, he is a poor, plodding sort of a creature, incapable of appreciating anything estimable beyond the pale of his own church, and quite ignorant of the world, of course. True, he may have travelled the earth over, and been conversant with men of every nation and every grade, but it is all the same. His views are so shockingly literal, — he is such an utter stranger to the rosy, refracting atmosphere surrounding men of taste, that it is evident even to persons whose observations of human nature have been necessarily bounded by the magic limits of '*our set*,' and whose travels have never extended beyond the streets of their native town, that he does not *know the world!*

But then he is to be respected *in a certain way;* for though he has spent the prime of his days in beating his head against a wall for the good of all mankind, he meant well, poor fellow! — and, without entering too deeply into the delicate subject of intellect, it may be boldly asserted, that his sympathies are limited only by his ignorance and prejudice.

Well, the big heart is some compensation for the shallow brain; and so I will venture to assure certain young persons, who read the Macedonian as a duty, and some other things as a pleasure, that there is no more ridiculous cant — *cant* is by no means peculiar to religion — in the wide world, than the pretty popular trash about unsophisticated nature. A poet was once disenchanted by seeing a 'great fat Circassian girl,' sitting on 'one of her heels,' 'devouring a pie;' and I dare say, the 'saucer-eyed' beauty had never performed a more intellectual, or indeed a more sentimental act in her life. I could certainly produce, from among my Burmese neighbors, a better subject for genius to waste itself upon, than the feather-girdled nymph of the woods, that a year or two since figured in a fashionable magazine, in the attitude of triumphing over a pair of sheepish looking missionaries; but excuse me from vouching for the capabilities of my *protégée* beyond the rice and curry line, save on great occasions, when her intellect might actually soar to the height of silks, face-powder — not *soap* — necklaces, and bangles. A sensible Burmese woman — one of our victims — told me, not long since, that previously to being taught by the missionaries, she knew as little of Boodhism as of Christianity. She supposed Gaudama was some old priest living somewhere on the hill, and thought it fine fun to turn out, with her young companions on worship days, to make offerings, and prostrate herself, in all her finery, before a pagoda; but for what purpose she went, it never once occurred to her to inquire. She had not the most distant conception of a future state, and could not recollect that she had ever once thought of death in connection with herself. In short, this woman, who is now as familiar with the Word of God as any Sunday scholar in America, was, at the age of twenty, but one remove above the brutes, 'a mere brute,' she styles herself; and she adds, that she does not think herself at all inferior to uneducated Burmese girls in general. But she was very pure and lovely, in her charming ignorance, was she not?—a sort of dew-gem in the wilderness? I do not know much about her girlhood, but of one thing I am quite certain, that the less said about it the better; for virtue is not forced upon Burmese women, as on those of some other eastern nations, by means of locks and bars, and mutilated guards. Since her marriage, it must be owned she has been quite a model woman, for this part of the world, having been found guilty of unfaithfulness in that relation but once; and then being able to prove, in self-defence, that she was under the influence of *arrack*—the Burmese substitute for *gin*. Do I write with such plainness as to shock the sensibilities of my readers? I do it unwillingly; and I assure them that I have dared to lift only the tiniest corner of the veil. But the wants and woes of the heathen must be more fully understood, before their condition can be materially improved. My happy, lovely sisters across the waters must know for whom they pray, and in whose behalf they make those sacrifices of personal elegancies, which will brighten their crowns in heaven. Not for some witching, fairy-like creature, who is robbed of half her charms by becoming a tame, simple-minded disciple of Christ; but for a degraded being, whose ignorance is surpassed only by her depravity, and whose personal habits would almost qualify her to furnish certain theorizing naturalists with the long desired link between man and his chattering caricature of the jungle.

'A law unto themselves,' argues our moralist, quoting the words of the first missionary, who left his own needy countrymen for the heathen; a rare auxiliary, by the way, in the good cause of showing up missionaries! 'A law unto themselves,' — and, secure in the strength of his supposed ally, he unhesitatingly seats himself in the commentator's chair. 'Throughout the whole chapter,' verses twelfth and sixteenth, for instance! — 'clearly shows, that if the Gentiles,' — ah! but that little *if!* it has ruined many a magnificent theory. Verily, expertness at concocting moral tales is not the best preparation in the world for a theologian. Another man, now, would have supposed that Paul's arguments 'clearly show' quite a different thing, or would, at least, have allowed him to be his own expositor. In the next chapter, the Gentile apostle, like the skilful reasoner that he was, gathers up his arguments in one hand, and while preparing to reach forth 'the law of faith' with the other, declares, 'We have before proved, both Jews and Gentiles, that they are all under sin.' ALL *under sin!* Ah, this is the unwelcome truth wrapped up in that mischievous, stubborn little IF, which *would* maintain its ground, though tolerably well disguised by false logic. So the Gentiles *do not* keep the 'law written on their hearts,' and they do need a gospel, after all. What! all of them? Cannot a single individual be found, who never violates the law of conscience? There are wonderful stories told of Socrates, — so wonderful, indeed, that many have believed his philosophy based on the revelation originally made to the Hebrews; while others are disposed to look with incredulity on perfections so enveloped in the haze of antiquity. Be that as it may, when a modern missionary finds the unique specimen of a Gentile, who 'does right, according to the law written on his heart,' the public will most certainly be made acquainted with the circumstance; for, indeed, such a miracle of a man would be a fortune to Mr. Barnum.

In sad and sober truth, the human being does not exist, who never transgresses both his own sense of right and the law of God. Every child of Adam has inherited a deadly poison, and he cherishes it because he loves it—delights in it—gloats over it. He knows, to a greater or less extent, that it is a vile thing, but he hugs it none the less closely for that; replying to all remonstrances, with the unanswerable argument of the New Zealand cannibal, when the missionary endeavored to dissuade him from eating human flesh, 'Oh, but it is *so* sweet!' An antidote to this fearful poison has been provided; it is within the reach of every soul in Christendom, and if he will not accept it, 'His blood be upon his own head,' not on that of the missionary who goes to the helpless, hopeless heathen. If a stubborn sick man refuse the draught that would restore him to health, shall all the doctors congregate about his bed, and leave a whole town to perish, for lack of the same specific? Oh, no, no; let bright, beautiful New York, sin-tarnished though she certainly is, pour forth her missionaries in crowds, and let all her fair sisters of the New World join in the noble enterprise. They will find that 'giving doth not impoverish;' but that he, who goes from among them in the faith of Christ, will leave a spirit behind him, which his personal presence could never have inspired. Let the daughter of luxury, in her home of refinement and purity, pause, and give a single moment to serious reflection. It would certainly be sweet to live there, and tread her rosy path daintily; but it would be glorious — oh, *so* glorious! to die, — for die she must even in her own bright home of love and beauty, — with the prayers and blessings of those she has rescued from the lowest depths of degradation, to precede her up to the throne of God. Let the young man, as he turns his back upon his *alma mater*, and contemplates taking his stand in a world of action, remember that he chooses not merely for time, but for eternity; and that results of incalculable magnitude are hanging on his decision. Let him remember that heaven sent forth the first Missionary — the Son of God — and he will not hesitate to think deeply, and pray fervently, over a profession which had such a glorious Founder. To what higher honor can a poor mortal aspire, than to be thus directly a co-worker with the Prince of glory? And is it not ennobling to the soul to be engaged, with a certainty of ultimate success, in the elevation of mighty nations? Is it not a sublime deed to reach forth the hand to a fallen spirit, and lift it to its place among the stars? Oh, the missionary enterprise! Its grandeur, its glory, is not yet half appreciated, even by its most enthusiastic advocates; for it is a theme that will tax the expanded intellects of the redeemed throughout the never-ending ages of eternity.

MINT, ANISE AND CUMMIN.

'Do you think it will do for —— to carry a silk umbrella in America?'

'Do! why?'

The sweet blue eyes, which had been lifted to mine in asking the first question, assumed a grave earnestness, as my gentle friend continued, 'I mean, will people make unpleasant remarks about it? Won't they think it not quite the thing for missionaries?'

I glanced at the poor, ricketty, carefully mended article in question, and answered truly, that I did not think it would be likely to create a very powerful sensation in America.

'Ah,' said my questioner, laughing, 'I see you don't understand these things. Now I would give a dozen umbrellas like this, for one good cotton one — of course I would. And yet

I have known missionaries to be censured for quite as innocent pieces of extravagance, (or economy,) as using this poor specimen of my handiwork, that you seem so inclined to ridicule.'

'And what if they are censured?'

'You remember what Paul says, "If meat cause my brother to offend, I will eat no flesh while the world standeth."'

'Ah, but ——' I spare the reader an exposition of Scripture, which might not tend to edification, and which was interrupted by the entrance of a third person.

'I am *so* glad you have come,' said my blue-eyed friend. 'Now don't you think this nice silk umbrella—see how carefully I have mended it—is quite as good as Mrs. ——'s gold watch?'

The two ladies laughed a short, curious, apologetic sort of a laugh, which had more of regret and pain, than mirth in it, but which served as an introduction to the story of the gold watch.

Mr. —— had been many years married, and had lived in tolerably easy circumstances, when he was converted, and received an appointment as a missionary to the heathen. Perhaps he thought Paul's prohibition of gold did not extend to anything so useful as a watch, or possibly he might have fancied that it had a strictly feminine application, or (what is most probable) he thought nothing at all about it; but certain it is that he carried his gold watch, now somewhat advanced in years, across the waters with him. In taking possession of the premises of a brother missionary about returning to America, the watch, as a matter of mutual accommodation, was exchanged for a clock, and so found its way again to its native shores. And now I must frankly acknowledge that my memory is at fault, as to precisely where the watch was lost, a circumstance which on the whole I do not regret, as it preserves me from a feeling of being on the road to personalities in making this little record. But the watch was lost by the missionary's wife, on her way to a female missionary meeting; and one of the ladies of the meeting kindly went in search of it. Being unsuccessful, she procured through a friend an advertisement to be inserted in a newspaper. And so it became known to the world, or to a certain portion of it, that 'a missionary' had lost a 'valuable gold watch.' And then my two friends, with a profusion of sorrowful smiles and sympathetic blushes, called on me to imagine the excitement in that little community! how every man, woman and child, not the actual proprietor of a gold watch (and some that were) declared that if it had come to this, if missionaries could afford such extravagances, they might get their money for the heathen as they could; *they* would never contribute a cent — not they, indeed!

'And how did it all end?' I inquired.

'Oh, it didn't end — such things never do. They go on increasing and doing mischief to the end of the chapter.'

'So you see,' said Blue-eyes, 'we cannot be too careful.'

'I see.' My answer was mechanical; for my thoughts were not there. They were busy recalling the image of a poor woman I once knew, who, while bearing the burden and heat of the day in the support of her family, was obliged to take especial care, lest, by some word or look, she should displease her husband; and so deprive herself of the occasional assistance he condescended to render. I, however, saw in a moment the infelicity of my comparison, for this man was a drunkard, not a professed child of God.

'We cannot be too careful,' repeated my gentle friend.

'Oh no.' I did not well know what to say, and I did not dare trust myself to look at her. Here was a tender young mother, bearing a heavier sorrow than those of my readers who have *only* laid their children beneath the sod know anything of; and in the midst of it all, troubling her meek thoughts about an old umbrella, lest she might inadvertently displease the men and women, who never in their lives made a real sacrifice for Christ. Not that she cared to please for her own sake — the very flush on her cheek told that—but from love to her Master she could submit to anything. And then my thoughts wandered off to snug, cozy homes, where dutiful children might gather, and even the *troubles* were of a comfortable, easy sort of character, rendering life more agreeable by occasional up-hill passages. And I saw in my musing (I could not help it) some of the occupants of these enviable homes, carping at the length of Peter's beard, or the fashion of John's mantle, while the Saviour of the world walked in all his majesty, unwelcomed, and scarcely recognised.

'It won't do!' at length I broke forth, more peremptorily than I had intended.

'You think it won't,' was the answer in a tone so resigned as to be positively touching.

'Oh, the old umbrella! I didn't mean that. It won't do for poor missionaries to trammel themselves with all these knotty consciences. You know "John came neither eating nor drinking, and they said he had a devil; the Son of Man came eating and drinking, and they said, Behold a gluttonous man, a wine-bibber," &c. I fancy the old generation is not quite extinct.'

'Oh, those were the unbelieving Jews — these are Christians.'

'You think so — well!' For a few days my thoughts were busy with those *Christians*, who 'bind heavy burdens and grievous to be borne' upon the shoulders of their brethren, and 'will not themselves so much as touch the burdens with one of their fingers.' But gradually the subject occupied less space in my mind, and finally came to be regarded as one of those phantoms which occasionally visit us during our daylight musings, as well as sleeping dreams. This state of confidence, however, was destined to be disturbed.

'And what do you think of my dress?' asked a returned missionary, at the close of a conversation in which she had been detailing certain plans of self-devotement to a friend. 'Pray do not look so surprised at my question, or I shall be quite ashamed. You must be aware that such things have more weight than they ought; and I should not wish my influence injured by anything so trivial.'

'You need not fear that; yours is just that happy style of dress which nobody ever sees. Now I take a second look, it is of fine material, but there is nothing showy about it; and as to fashion, it is neither quite new, nor so old as to attract attention by its oddity. A very fair specimen of the wearer's good sense and good taste both, it strikes me.'

'Indeed the wearer deserves no such compliment. I was quite shivering in New York, when Mrs. —— was so very kind as to present me with her last year's bonnet and mantle. They are, of course, nicer than I should have bought, but they are very comfortable; and I did not feel at liberty to refuse the gift, unless, indeed, I should do harm by wearing it. I should rather go back to my thin old shawl and straw bonnet, than have my nice, comfortable clothing stand in the way of my doing good.'

'I do not doubt that; but you need have no fears.'

Unfortunately this well-meaning friend was mistaken. The missionary went from place to place, pressing her cause, with an eloquent earnestness, which belongs to the deep, unselfish heart of a truly devoted woman; and while many listened prayerfully and contributed liberally, others (not mockers, not giddy women of the world, not declared enemies of the cause of missions) sat taking an inventory of her dress, estimating how many yards of cloth were in her mantle, and, in the course of their examinations, arriving at the astounding conclusion, that it was composed of as fine — possibly finer material than their own.

Out upon the woman! Did she presume to come, in all her finery, begging of them! They always had a good many doubts about this missionary business, but this — this was a little too much! And so these people kept back the accustomed sixpence — very likely to increase the fineness of their own mantles another winter. Perhaps not, though. Perhaps they would not wear a fine mantle, if it were given them. Perhaps they are very exact (as they ought to be) about the tithe of mint, anise and cummin; dressing in chintz, and eschewing ribands, altogether. And so they save their money — for what? To 'pull down their barns and build greater?' To add that long coveted lot to the farm? To provide for the possible wants of children, who have strong hands and able heads?

I will not ask for what; no matter what, if they 'neglect the weightier matters of the law.'

Now I am no defender of gold watches, or

silk umbrellas. I have no desire to varnish over the faults or follies of any missionary; but wo to that man who shall make the delinquencies of his brother-servant an excuse for disobeying the Master! Wo to that disciple of the Lord Jesus Christ, who, under any pretext whatever, refuses to obey the last command of his risen Redeemer, to the very best of his ability! If he cannot himself 'go,' he *must* procure a substitute, or assist in procuring one, at his peril. Assist, not meanly and parsimoniously, serving God, as somebody has it, by sixpences, but with a noble generosity, worthy of his character as a Christian, worthy of the wondrous commission with which he has been honored, worthy of the glorious cause of his all-glorious King.

THE MISSIONARY.

One blossom in his path uncloses,
  His prayers its sun, his tears its rain,
A flower Eve found not with the roses
  Of her bright silver-fringed domain.
One joy beneath his foot upsprings,
Extracted from the serpent's stings:—
As the soiled wing, enchained to earth,
  Its thraldom bursts, and soaring, flies,
So wakes the soul to its new birth,
  And bounds, exulting, to the skies.
To loose the prisoned flutterer's wing,
Touch the degraded spirit's spring,
To give a songster to the sky,
A voice to swell the choir on high,—
Oh, if there be for man a bliss,
Above what angels feel, 'tis this!

BODAU-PARAH.

Persons in the least familiar with Burmese history must have heard of the already half-fabulous feats of that mighty conqueror and deliverer, the justly famed Alompra.* They will have heard of his bold and successful venture to obtain freedom from Peguan bondage; of his bravery in battle, of his wisdom in council, and how, through him, the proud Burmans took for a time their former rank among the great nations of the East. The Burmans determined utterly to crush the nation that had dared to make them slaves; and accordingly, the whole Peguan dynasty, every person suspected of having a drop of royal blood in his

* English corruption of Aloung-parah, — a name given after death, in allusion to the body's having lain in regal state in the Martaban valley.

veins, embracing the flower of the nobility, suffered death by starvation, by strangling, or by the more honored medium of the river and the crimson sack. The imperial crown, of course, fell upon the brow of the nation's deliverer; and, half-deified as he was, his laws must needs be sacred for centuries to come. Among other regulations, of more or less wisdom and importance, he established a new order of succession to the throne. Being the eldest of several brothers, he ordained that his crown should descend through each of the surviving brothers successively to his own eldest son; and then again through a family of brothers, back to the eldest son of the eldest. Alompra no doubt intended to make a wise and politic arrangement, which should insure to the throne men of mature judgment, and prevent the horrors of a regency in such a country. But his plan was a total failure. Through the agency of ambitious brothers, and elder sons impatient of delay, it has occasioned so much bloodshed and confusion, that it may justly be considered one of the principal causes of the rapid deterioration so evident in the national character of the Burmese.

The youngest son of Alompra survived not only his uncles and brothers, but his own children, leaving the throne to a favorite grandson. For this cause he is always spoken of as Bodau-parah, or the royal grandfather. This man possessed, with a thoughtful, and somewhat philosophic turn of mind, great strength of will, pride, sternness, and a lofty self-reliance, which his ruggedness and force of character redeemed from the ridiculous vanity of his successor of 'golden fetter' memory, and even elevated into something like sublimity. His name is now most reverently cherished throughout Burmah, as the embodiment of all that is daring and noble; and the taint of religious heresy, which at one time threatened the ruin of his character, is resolutely denied or forgotten. If a stranger should wish to awaken a glow of patriotism in a Burman, that would beautify his plain but intellectual face, (taking care that he be not of Peguan origin,) he has only to call up some grateful reminiscence of Bodau-parah.

The following incident relative to an attempt

on the part of the English, to establish a commercial treaty between the two countries during the reign of Bodau, was related to me by my fine-spirited old teacher, a pure Burman, who had worn the yellow robe at Ava, and who, although an exile for his religion, still kept a feeling of loyalty at his heart, fed by all the proud fire of his race.

THE KING AND THE ENVOY.

Proud the monarch in his palace,
  In his golden palace sat,
Girt as with the borealis,
  Sandalled foot on jewelled mat.
Slaves to him and his opinions,
  Swart old courtiers round him knelt;
And throughout his broad dominions,
  Even his slightest nod was felt.

Now there bowed a courtly stranger,
  Fair of face and smooth of speech;—
'If—oh, glorious king, if danger
  To the golden foot should reach,
Owns thy brother power unbounded;
  On the winds his tall ships fly;
Where his thunders have resounded,
  Foes like jungle-blossoms lie.

Then the old king slowly baring
  One dark, brawny, sinewy arm;
As a gladiator daring
  Man and beast to work him arm;
Stretched it to the wondering Briton,
  Stretched it with a scornful laugh, —
'*Kyee-san, nen* * should foes dare threaten,
  Burmah needs no foreign staff!'

Wild eyes gleamed, proud words were uttered,
  Bearded lips with smiles were gay;
Low the baffled stranger muttered,
  As he turned and strode away:
Like the gull, her white wings spreading,
  Seaward wheeled his barque once more;
Restless feet her fair decks treading,
  Dark eyes laughing from the shore.

But there is another anecdote of Bodau-parah, which, though no less truthful or interesting than the above, it is a scandal to repeat in Burmah.

For a period of more than two thousand years Boodhism had prevailed uninterrupedly. Introduced right royally, and through a royal medium

---

* Look [at this] — you!

from India, the work of propagation among the common people had been followed up by missionaries from Ceylon, till probably no national religion under the sun ever so claimed the undivided affections and convictions of an entire nation. Supported on the one hand by the absolute authority of an uncompromising monarchy, and on the other by the powerful influence of a priesthood, whose roots extended into every family of respectability, drawing no stinted nourishment from family pride; a structure really admirable in itself, still stood forth without a fracture, and with only a slight mantling of moss and mildew to mar its beauty. While this comparatively pure and elevated faith had been supplanted in its original dominions by the disgusting doctrines and horrible practices of the Brahminists, while in China it held a divided sovereignty, in Thibet had become so changed in character as to be scarcely recognisable, and even in its old Cinghalese home had deteriorated almost to a level with surrounding idolatries, in Burmah it had only swerved a little from its original simplicity, and gathered a few premonitory stains. True, the priests did not obey, in spirit, the command of Gaudama, to go clothed in rags, but their rich silken robes were sewed together from such nominal fragments as would bring them within the letter of the law; and though they adhered to the original rule of owning no property, and striving for no political power, they ruled with absolute sway over commoners and nobility, and rich communities of leprous beggars were their obsequious bankers. In one thing they had gone counter to the commands of Gaudama. They had been forbidden to inhabit monasteries within the limits of the town, an injunction which had been from time immemorial practically forgotten. But the worst blot upon the Boodhistic religion, the most destructive of its purity, and the most degrading in its influence on the character of the people was *nät*, or spirit-worship. Little altars to both good and evil spirits were often erected at the very doors of the *Kyoungs;* and the younger priests not infrequently shared their quota of rice with these invisible visitors, while the older ones winked at the folly. To a still more alarming extent was this demoralizing practice carried on among the people.

The great distinctive feature of Boodhism is its proclaiming *one god*, who alone (through images of himself, pagodas erected over his relics, and the priests who devote themselves to his honor) is the suitable object of worship. A belief in a plurality of gods always has the effect of degrading a people — a truth trite enough in our ears, but one which the thoughtful Bodau-parah had occupied years in arriving at. In fact, the stern king had had too long a term of peace for the good of old institutions; and during this term of peace, he had thought, and observed, and delved in old Pali books, till he became more learned in both the philosophy and mythology of Boodhism, than even the priests themselves. He had compared and pondered, till his shrewd mind had arrived at many startling conclusions; and, bold man as he was, he expressed his opinions so freely, that his most politic nobles trembled for what they well knew to be the glory of the nation; his more reckless courtiers grew openly and gayly irreligious; while troubled priests, in the recesses of their monasteries, laid a finger on their lips significantly, and sighed, rather than whispered, '*päramät.*'* In the meantime the governors of different provinces seemed aware that the most effectual mode of courting royal favor was to hold the reins of religious intolerance slackly; and latitudinous opinions, and freedom of inquiry spread throughout the empire with wonderful rapidity. In this newly opened nursery of thought, sprang up innumerable sects, or schools of philosophy. There were men who denied the existence of matter; men who insisted that matter was only a development of mind; and those who maintained, with innumerable shades of difference, directly the reverse of this proposition. There were deists of a dozen different schools; and transcendentalists, who ventured farther into the realms of mysticism, than the more practical occidental mind would dare, or has the spiritual capacity to go. Among these free-thinking philosophers was a noble old patriarch living at Prome, who, according to all accounts, must have been a modern Socrates, and who, in the

* Infidel.

reign of the Grandson, became a still closer imitator of the ancient sage, by sacrificing his life to his faith. Another was Moung Shwayngōng, a man of commanding personal presence, and exalted character, who, with several of his disciples, afterwards embraced Christianity, and contributed to give a cast of uncommon intellectuality to the first Christian Church in Burmah. One of his followers, (probably the only survivor) an old lady now living in Maulmain, invariably attracts the attention of strangers, by her singular refinement and elegance of manner, her general intelligence, and her genuine Christian graces. And yet she is said to have been, at the time of her conversion, far from a brilliant specimen of the intellectual coterie to which she belonged.

At length Bodau-parah, having very unintentionally thrown open the flood-gates of thought throughout his realm, took the alarm. He never had the least intention of allowing such latitude of opinion to common minds ; and he devoted himself with characteristic energy to finding a remedy. There were men of almost all nations assembled at Ava, and he resolved to have, through their aid, an examination of the different religions, in order that Burmah might adopt the wisest code. Royal councillors and aristocratic priests trembled; but they dared not manifest their uneasiness by a murmur. The haughty king asked no adviser, and he constituted himself sole judge. The day was appointed; the various representatives came together; the royal secretaries sat down with their black books spread before them; and the king conducted the examination in person, and sometimes, in his earnestness, without the formality of an interpreter. There was the wily Brahmin, telling on his rosary the names of his multitude of uncouth divinities; the exiled Parsee, with his finely cut features, and deep, melancholy eyes, in which slumbered a fire as fervid as that he worshipped; the bearded Moslem, who hid the Son of God behind the shadow of his mighty human Prophet; and the Armenian and Romanist, who also hid from the poor heathen king, the Saviour of the world, but, for the conquering Prophet, substituted a woman.

And were these all? Were Armenian merchants and Portuguese Padrés the only representatives of the Christian religion in Burmah? Oh, 'how unsearchable are His judgments, and His ways past finding out?' Not far from the mouth of that same Irrawaddy, whose crystal tide swept down the white sands of the golden city, sat the first American missionary, pointing dumbly to the different objects in his room, and writing down their names as indicated in the strange accents of the teacher by his side. And while, with his heroic wife, his longing heart often turned toward the place, where, years afterward, one received 'in his body the marks of the Lord Jesus' to wear till death, and the other gathered up the seeds of martyrdom; it was well for their peace, for their faith, perhaps, that they could not divine the scene passing there at that moment. It would have appeared to them a golden opportunity lost forever.

But there was one man at Ava calling himself a Protestant. A large framed man, with coarse, strongly marked features, and ruddy complexion, though wearing the Burman dress, answered to an English name. It was reported that for some crime, which rumor variously represented, though she never wiped it from blood-guiltiness, this man had escaped from the English navy, and taken shelter under a heathen government, adopting with the dress, the manners, customs, and, as far as in his power, the character of the people. He had not troubled himself about religion, and in a time of such general laxness of opinion, he had not of course been troubled. This man, with probably some effort to recall his mother's teachings, and now and then prompted by the Spanish merchant at his side to whom we are indebted for the story, at last succeeded in repeating the ten commandments! And that was all. The representatives of the different religions left the royal presence; and not the faintest whisper of the gospel of Christ had fallen on the ear of the inquiring monarch.

The king hastily retired to the inner palace alone; while ministers of state, and gallant court favorites, gathered here and there in little knots, to discuss the wonders of the day. Subtle metaphysicians enlarged upon the spiritual doctrines of the Parsee; gay, showy young men compared sneeringly the pomp of any Moorman festival, with the gorgeous splendors of a Boodhistic cremation of priests; the court wit perpetrated an epigram on woman-worship; while sober politicians attempted to weigh the effect of the whole proceeding upon the prosperity of the country. It was evident to all that the monarch was disappointed, chagrined; but none but the Almighty saw, or could guess, the workings of his dark, though powerful mind. At length, after three days, he came forth in great state, and proclaimed the Boodhistic faith to be the most elevated, the purest in the world, and the only one worthy the attention of Burmans. The shouts that rose beyond the magic circle of the king's personal attendants were almost deafening; and scarcely a voice in the golden city but joined in the general cry, ascribing half the attributes of Deity to the mighty son of Alompra. But soon the cry died away in consternation; for the king had yet other communications to make, and edicts to issue. As Boodhism was a pure religion, he determined it should be observed in its purity. All the *nät* tables were ordered to be torn down; and *nät* offerings and *nät* worship forbidden, on penalty of imprisonment and final death. *Kyoungs* erected within the limits of the town were dismantled; and the priests stripped of their rich robes, and driven back to the wilderness. Then ensued a scene of confusion. Many priests, especially those of high family, resisted, and were thrown into prison. Many concealed their sacred garments under the plaided cloth of a layman, wound a turban around their shaven crowns, and fled to Prome, to Rangoon, and even across a section of the bay to Martaban, Kyaikamee, or Bike, being everywhere protected by the trembling, sympathizing people. One of these fugitives actually obtained a shelter for the night, and a protection for his effects, in the house of the American missionary at Rangoon; who heard of the persecution only as the cruel and causeless act of a despotic monarch, and never dreamed that it could be the work of a mind apparently ripe for the reception of the gospel.

Gradually the king relaxed in the energy of his measures, and affairs began very slowly to resume their former position. But before much had been accomplished, he died, and left the throne to his grandson; who promptly restored the old order of things, with no scruples respecting undue pomp and glitter. And the result, under him and his successors, is well known to the Christian world.

'Oh, if you could only, *only* have been there!' was the exclamation of the listener to this tale. 'Even a few words might have been sufficient.'

The narrator answered with a quiet, but expressive smile.

'If you could *only* have known!'

'I felt as you do when Lanciego first told me the circumstance, when we were chained together in the death prison at Ava; but God cares for the interests of his kingdom far better than the wisest and best of us know how to care. The religion of our Saviour, propagated by despotism, would be a curse, and not a blessing to a nation. And even the favoring smile of royalty is a thing I have long since ceased to pray for. All we want of any government is bare toleration — that is, to be let alone. It is contrary to the very spirit of Christianity to begin with those in power, and work downward; and when it does so begin, the vital spark is sure to escape in the process. Christ, our pattern, began low. He did not turn away from Nicodemus, or the Roman centurion, or the nobleman; but he made no special effort for the benefit of those classes, with the view of gaining, through them, greater influence over the lower orders. Missionaries, if they would be successful, must have more faith in God; and work in his own appointed way, *preaching the gospel to the poor.* It is painful to think of the pitiable old king, groping so earnestly, in his darkness; but the Saviour has the good of Burmah infinitely nearer his heart than we have, and He was watching when my poor "eyes were holden." I thank Him for His care; and I stand ready to do His work, however lowly, and wait His time, however long.'

DEATH OF BOARDMAN.

PALE with sickness, weak and worn,
Is the Christian hero borne,
Over hill, and brook, and fen,
By his band of swart, wild men,
Dainty odors floating back,
From their blossom-crushing track.

Through the jungle vast and dim,
Swells out Nature's matin hymn:
Bulbuls 'mid the berries red,
Showers of mellow music shed;
Thrushes 'neath their crimson hoods,
Chant their loves along the woods;

And the heron, as he springs
Up, with startled rush of wings,

Joins the gorgeous peacock's scream;
While the gushing of the stream
Gives sweet cadence to the hymn,
Swelling through the jungle dim.

So they bear him on his way,
Till the sunless sky is gray;
Then within some lone zayat,
Gentle fingers spread the mat;
And a watcher, sad and wan,
Bends above him till the dawn.

Up and on! The tangled brake
Hides the deadly water-snake;
And the tiger, from his lair
Half up-springing, snuffs the air,
Doubtful gazing where they pass,
Trailing through the long wet grass.

Day has faded, — rosy dawn
Blushed again o'er wood and lawn;
Day has deepened, — level beams
Light the brook in changeful gleams,
Breaking in a golden flood,
Round strange groupings in the wood.

There, where mountains wild and high,
Range their peaks along the sky,
Lo! they pause. A crimson glow
Burns upon that cheek of snow;
And within the eyes' soft blue
Quiver tears like drops of dew.

Upward, from the wooded dell,
High the joyous greetings swell,
Peal on peal; then, circling round,
Turbaned heads salute the ground,
While upon the dewy air
Floats a faint, soft voice in prayer.

With the fever on his cheek,
Breathing forth his teachings meek,
Long the gospel-bearer lies,
Till the stars have climbed the skies,
And the young moon's slender rim
Hides behind the mountain grim.

'Twas for this sweet boon he came,
Crushing back Death's eager claim;
Yet a few more lambs to fold,
Ere he mingles with the mould,—

Lambs with torn and crimsoned fleece,
Wildered in this wilderness.

Once again the golden day
Drops her veil of silver gray;
And that dark-eyed mountain band
Print with bare, brown feet the sand,
Or the crystal wave turn back,
Rippling from their watery track.

Meekly down the river's bed,
Sire and son alike are led,
Parting the baptismal flood,
As of old in Judah's wood;
While throughout the sylvan glen
Rings the stern, deep-voiced Amen.

With the love-light in his eyes,
Mute the dying teacher lies.
It is finished. Bear him back!
Haste along the jungle track!
See the lid uplifting now, —
See the glory on his brow.

It is finished. Wood and glen
Sigh their mournful, meek Amen.

'Mid that circle, sorrow-spanned,
Clasping close an icy hand,
Lo! the midnight watcher wan,
Waiting yet another dawn.

WAYSIDE PREACHING.

The sunlight fell aslant upon the fragile frame-work of a Burman zayat; but though it was some hours past mid-day, the burning rays were not yet level enough to look too intrusively beneath the low, projecting eaves. Yet the day was intensely hot, and the wearied occupant of the one bamboo chair in the centre of the building, looked haggard and care-worn. All day long had he sat in that position, repeating over and over again, as he could find listeners, such simple truths as mothers are accustomed to teach the infant on their knee; and now his head was aching, and his heart was very heavy. He had met some scoffers, some who seemed utterly indifferent, but not one sincere inquirer after truth.

In the middle of the day, when the sun was hottest, and scarcely a European throughout all

India was astir, he had received the greatest number of visitors; for the passers-by were glad of a moment's rest and shelter from the sun. The mats were still spread invitingly upon the floor; but though persons of almost every description were continually passing and repassing, they seemed each intent on his own business, and the missionary was without a listener. He thought of his neglected study-table at home, of his patient, fragile wife, toiling through the numerous cares of the day alone, of the letters his friends were expecting, and which he had no time to write, of the last periodicals from his dear native land, lying still unread; and every little while, between the other thoughts, came real pinings after a delicious little book of devotion, which he had slid into his pocket in the morning, promising it his first moment of leisure. Then he was, naturally, an active man, of quick, ardent temperament, and with such views of the worth of time as earnest American men can scarcely fail to gain; and it went to his heart to lose so many precious moments. If he could only do something to fill up these tedious intervals! But no; this was a work to which he must not give a divided mind. He was renewing a half-tested experiment in wayside preaching, and he would not suffer his attention to be distracted by anything else. While his face was hidden by his book, and his mind intent on self-improvement, some poor passer-by might lose a last, an only opportunity of hearing the words of life. To be sure, his own soul seemed very barren, and needed refreshing; and his body was weary — wearied well nigh to fainting, more with the dull, palsying inanity of the day's fruitless endeavors, than with anything like labor. Heavily beat down the hot sun, lighting up the amber-like brown of the thatch, as with a burning coal; while thickly in its broad rays floated a heavy golden cloud of dust and motes, showing in what a wretched atmosphere the delicate lungs were called to labor. Meantime, a fever-freighted breeze, which had been, all the hot day, sweeping the effluvia from eastern marshes, stirred the glossy leaves of the orange-tree across the way, and parched the lip, and kindled a crimson spot upon the wan cheek of the weary missionary.

'God reigns,' he repeated, as though some reminder of the sort were necessary. 'God Almighty reigns; and I have given myself to him, soul and body, for time and for eternity. His will be done!' Still, how long the day seemed! How broad the space that blistering sun had yet to travel, before its waiting, its watching, and its laboring would be ended! Might he not indulge himself just one moment? His hand went to his pocket, and the edge of a little book peeped forth a moment, and then, with a decided push, was thrust back again. No; he would not trifle with his duty. He would be sternly, rigidly faithful; and the blessing would surely come in time. Yet it was with an irrepressible yawn that he took up a little Burman tract prepared by himself, of which every word was as familiar as his own name, and commenced reading aloud. The sounds caught the ear of a coarsely clad water-bearer, and she lowered the vessel from her head, and seated herself afar off, just within the shadow of the low eaves. Attracted by the foreign accent of the reader, few passed without turning the head a few moments to listen; then catching at some word which seemed to them offensive, they would repeat it mockingly and hasten on.

Finally the old water-bearer, grinning in angry derision till her wrinkled visage became positively hideous, rose, slowly adjusted the earthen vessel on her head, and passed along, muttering as she went, 'Jesus Christ! — no Nigban! — ha, ha, ha!' The heart of the missionary sunk within him, and he was on the point of laying down the book. But the shadow of another passer-by fell upon the path, and he continued a moment longer. It was a tall, dignified looking man, leading by the hand a boy, the open mirthfulness of whose bright, button-like eyes was in perfect keeping with his dancing little feet. The stranger was of a grave, staid demeanor, with a turban of aristocratic smallness, sandals turning up at the toe, a silken robe of somewhat subdued colors, and a snow-white tunic of gentlemanlike length, and unusual fineness.

'Papa, papa!' said the boy, with a merry little skip, and twitching at the hand he was holding, 'Look, look, papa! *there* is Jesus Christ's man. *Amai!* how shockingly white!'

'Jesus Christ's man' raised his eyes from the book which he could read just as well without eyes, and bestowed one of his brightest smiles upon the little stranger, just as the couple were passing beyond the corner of the zayat, but not too late to catch a bashfully pleased recognition. The father did not speak nor turn his head, but a ray of sunshine went down into the missionary's heart from those happy little eyes; and he somehow felt that his hour's reading had not been thrown away. He had remarked this man before, in other parts of the town; and had striven in various ways to attract his attention, but without success. He was evidently known, and most probably avoided; but the child, with that shy, pleased, half-confiding, roguish sort of smile, seemed sent as an encouraging messenger. The missionary continued his reading with an increase of earnestness and emphasis. A priest wrapped his yellow robes about him and sat down upon the steps, as though for a moment's rest. Then, another stranger came up boldly, and with considerable ostentation seated himself on the mat. He proved to be a philosopher, from the school then recently disbanded at Prome; and he soon drew on a brisk, animated controversy.

The missionary did not finish his day's work with the shutting up of the zayat. At night, in his closet, he remembered both philosopher and priest; pleaded long and earnestly for the scoffing old water-bearer; and felt a warm tear stealing to his eye, as he presented the case of the tall stranger, and the laughing, dancing ray of sunshine at his side.

Day after day went by, as oppressively hot, as dusty, and bringing as many feverish winds as ever; but the hours were less wearisome, because many little buds of hope had been fashioned, which might yet expand into perfect flowers. But every day the tall stranger carried the same imperturbable face past the zayat; and every day the child made some silent advance towards the friendship of the missionary, bending his half-shaven head, and raising his little nut-colored hand to his forehead, by way of salutation, and smiling till his round face dimpled all over like ripples in a sunny pool.

One day, as the pair came in sight, the missionary beckoned with his hand, and the child, with a single bound, came to his knee.

'Moung-Moung!' exclaimed the father in a tone of surprise blended with anger. But the child was back again in a moment, with a gay colored Madras handkerchief wound around his head; and with his bright lips parted, his eyes sparkling, and dancing with joy, and his face wreathed with smiles, he seemed the most charming thing in nature. '*Tai hlah-the!*' (very beautiful) said the child, touching his new turban, and looking into his father's clouded face, with the fearlessness of an indulged favorite.

'*Tai hlah-the!*' repeated the father involuntarily. He meant the child.

'You have a very fine boy there, Sir,' said the missionary, in a tone intended to be conciliatory. The stranger turned with a low salaam. For a moment he seemed to hesitate, as though struggling between his native politeness and his desire to avoid an acquaintance with the proselyting foreigner. Then taking the hand of the little boy who was too proud and happy to notice his father's confusion, he hastened away.

'I do not think that zayat a very good place to go to, Moung-Moung,' said the father gravely, when they were well out of hearing. The boy answered only by a look of inquiry strangely serious for such a face as his.

'These white foreigners are ——.' He did not say what, but shook his head with mysterious meaning. The boy's eyes grew larger and deeper, but he only continued to look up into his father's face in wondering silence.

'I shall leave you at home to-morrow, to keep you from his wicked sorceries.'

'Papa!'

'What, my son?'

'I think it will do no good to leave me at home.'

'Why?'

'He has done something to me.'

'Who? the *Kalah-byoo?*'

'I do not think he has hurt me, papa; but I cannot — keep — away — no — oh, no!'

'What do you mean, Moung-Moung?'

'The sorcerer has done something to me — put his beautiful eye on me. I see it *now.*'

And the boy's own eyes glowed with a strange, startling brilliancy.

''*Mai, 'mai!* what a boy! *He* is not a sorcerer, only a very provoking man. His eye, — whish! It is nothing to my little Moung-Moung. I was only sporting. But we will have done with him; you shall go there no more ——'

'If I can help it, papa!'

'Help it! Hear the foolish child! What strange fancies!'

'Papa!'

'What, my son?'

'You will not be angry?'

'Angry!' The soft smile on that stern bearded face was a sufficient answer.

'Is it true that she — my mother ——?'

'Hush, Moung-Moung!'

'Is it true that she ever *shikoed* to the Lord Jesus Christ?'

'Who dares to tell you so?'

'I must not say, papa; the one who told me, said it was as much as life is worth to talk of such things to *your* son. Did she, papa?'

'What did he mean? Who could have told you such a tale?'

'Did she, papa?'

'That is a very pretty *goung-boung* the foreigner gave you.'

'Did she?'

'And makes your bright eyes brighter than ever.'

'Did my mother *shiko* to the Lord Jesus Christ?'

'There, there, you have talked enough, my boy,' said the father gloomily; and the two continued their walk in silence. As the conversation ceased, a woman who, with a palm-leaf fan before her face, had followed closely in the shadow of the stranger — so closely, indeed, that she might have heard every word that had been spoken — stopped at a little shop by the way, and was soon seemingly intent on making purchases.

'Ko Shway-bay!' called out the missionary. A man bearing a large satchel, which he had just newly filled with books, appeared at the door of an inner apartment of the zayat.

''*Ken-payah !*'

'Did you observe the tall man who just passed, leading a little boy?'

'I saw him.'

'What do you know about him?'

'He is a writer under government — a very respectable man — haughty — reserved ——'

'And what else?'

'He hates — Christians, *Tsayah*.'

'Is he very bigoted, then?'

'No, *Tsayah;* he is more like a *päramät* than a Boodhist. Grave as he appears, he sometimes treats sacred things very playfully, always carelessly. But does the teacher remember — it may be now three, four — I do not know how many years ago, — a young woman came for medicine ——?'

The missionary smiled. 'I should have a wonderful memory, Shway-bay, if I carried all my applicants for medicine in it.'

'But this one was not like other women. She had the face of a *nät-thamee*,' [goddess or angel,] 'and her voice — the teacher *must* remember her voice — it was like the silvery chimes of the pagoda bells at midnight. She was the favorite wife of the *Sah-ya*, and this little boy, her only child, was very ill. She did not dare ask you to the house, or even send a servant for the medicine, for her husband was one of the most violent persecutors ——'

'Ay, I do recollect her, by her distress and her warm gratitude. So this is her child! What has become of the mother?'

'Has the teacher forgotten putting a Gospel of Matthew in her hand, and saying that it contained medicine for *her*, for that she was afflicted with a worse disease than the fever of her little son; and then lifting up his hands and praying very solemnly?'

'I do not recall the circumstance just now. But what came of it?'

'They say,' answered the Burman, lowering his voice, and first casting an investigating glance around him, —'they say that the medicine cured her.'

'Ah!'

'She read the book nights, while watching by her baby, and then she would kneel down and pray as the teacher had done. At last the *Sah-ya* got the writing.'

'What did he do with it?'

'Only burnt it. But she was a tender little creature, and could not bear his look; so, as the baby got out of danger, she took the fever——'

'And died?' asked the missionary, remarking some hesitation in the manner of his narrator.

'Not of the fever altogether.'

'What then? Surely, *he* did not——'

'No, *Tsayah!* it must have been an angel-call. The *Sah-ya* was very fond of her, and did everything to save her; but she just grew weaker, day after day, and her face more beautiful; and there was no holding her back. She got courage as she drew near Paradise, and begged the *Sah-ya* to send for you. He is not a hard-hearted man, and she was more than life and soul to him; but he would not send. And so she died, talking to the last moment of the Lord Jesus Christ, and calling on everybody about her to love Him, and worship none but Him.'

'Is this true, Shway-bay?'

'*I* know nothing about it, *Tsayah;* and it is not very safe to know anything. The *Sah-ya* has taken an oath to destroy everybody having too good a memory. But,'—and the man again looked cautiously around him, — 'does the teacher think that little Burman children are likely to run into the arms of foreigners, without being taught?'

'Aha! say you so, Shway-bay?'

'I say nothing, *Tsayah*.'

'What of the child?'

'A wonderful boy, *Tsayah*. He seems usually as you have seen him; but he has another look, — so strange! He must have caught something from his mother's face, just before she went up to the golden country.'

The missionary seemed lost in thought; and the assistant, after waiting a moment to be questioned farther, slung his satchel over his shoulder, and proceeded up the street.

The next day the missionary remarked that the *Sah-ya* went by on the other side of the way, and without the little boy; and the next day, and the next the same. In the meantime, the wrinkled old water-bearer had become a sincere inquirer. 'The one shall be taken and the other left,' sighed the missionary, as he tried to discern the possible fate of his bright-eyed little friend.

The fourth day came. The old water-bearer was in an agitated state of joy and doubt—a timid, but true believer. The self-confident philosopher had almost ceased to cavil. Fresh inquirers had appeared, and the missionary's heart was strengthened. 'It is dull work,' he said to himself, though without any expression of dullness in his face; 'but it is the Saviour's own appointed way, and the way the Holy Spirit will bless.' Then his thoughts turned to the stern *Sah-ya*, and his little boy; and he again murmured, with more of dejection in his manner than when he had spoken of the dullness of the work, 'And the other left—the other left!'

The desponding words had scarcely passed his lips, when, with a light laugh, the very child who was in his thoughts, and who somehow clung so tenaciously to his heart, sprang up the steps of the zayat, followed by his grave, dignified father. The boy wore his new Madras turban, arranged with a pretty sort of jauntiness, and above its showy folds he carried a red lacquered tray, with a cluster of golden plantains on it. Placing the gift at the missionary's feet, he drew back, with a pleased smile of boyish shyness, while the man, bowing courteously, took his seat upon the mat.

'Sit down, Moung-Moung, sit down,' said the father, in the low tone that American parents use when reminding careless little boys of their hats; for though Burmans and Americans differ somewhat in their peculiar notions of etiquette, the children of both races seem equally averse to becoming learners.

'You are the foreign priest,' he remarked civilly, and more by way of introduction than inquiry.

'I am a missionary.'

The stranger smiled, for he had purposely avoided the offensive epithet; and was amused and conciliated by the missionary's frank use of it. 'And so you make people believe in Jesus Christ?'

'I try to.'

The visitor laughed outright; then, as if a little ashamed of his rudeness, he composed his features, and with his usual courtesy resumed, 'My little son has heard of you, Sir; and he is very anxious to learn something about Jesus

Christ. It is a pretty story that you tell of that man — prettier I think than any of our fables; and you need not be afraid to set it forth in its brightest colors; for my Moung-Moung will never see through its absurdity, of course.'

The missionary threw a quick, scrutinizing glance on the face of his visitor. He saw that the man was ill at ease, that his carelessness was entirely assumed, and that underneath all, there was a deep, wearing anxiety, which he fancied was in some way connected with his boy. 'Ah! you think so? To what particular story do you allude?'

'Why that of the strange sort of being you call Jesus Christ, — a *nät*, or prince or something of that sort, — dying for us poor fellows, and so — ha, ha! The absurdity of the thing makes me laugh; though there is something in it beautiful too. Our stupid *pongyees* would never have thought out anything one half so fine; and the pretty fancy has quite enchanted little Moung-Moung here.'

'I perceive you are a *päramät*,' said the missionary. 'No, — oh no; I am a true and faithful worshipper of Lord Gaudama; but of course neither you nor I subscribe to all the fables of our respective religions. There is quite enough that is honest and reasonable in our Boodhistic system to satisfy me; but my little son' (here the father seemed embarrassed, and laughed again, as though to cover his confusion,) 'is bent on philosophical investigation—eh, Moung-Moung?'

'But are you not afraid that my teachings will do the child harm?'

The visitor looked up with a broad smile of admiration, as though he would have said, 'You are a very honest fellow, after all;' then regarding the child with a look of mingled tenderness and apprehension, he said softly, 'Nothing can harm little Moung-Moung, Sir.'

'But what if I should tell you I do believe every thing I preach, as firmly as I believe you sit on the mat before me; and that it is the one desire of my life to make everybody else believe it—you and your child among the rest?'

The *Sah-ya* tried to smile, tried to looked unconcerned; but his easy nonchalance of manner seemed utterly to forsake him in his need; and finally abandoning the attempt to renew his former tone of banter, he answered quietly, 'I have heard of a writing you possess, which, by your leave, I will take home and read to Moung-Moung.'

The missionary selected a little tract from the parcel on the table beside him, and extended it to his visitor. '*Sah-ya*,' said he, solemnly, 'I herewith put into your hands the key to eternal life and happiness. This active, intelligent soul of yours, with its exquisite perception of moral beauty and loveliness,' and he glanced toward the child, 'cannot be destined to inhabit a dog, a monkey, or a worm, in another life. God made it for higher purposes; and I hope and pray that I may yet meet you, all beautiful, and pure, and glorious, in a world beyond the reach of pain or death, and above all, beyond the reach of sin.'

Up to this time the boy had sat upon his mat like a statue of silence; his usually dancing eyes fixed steadfastly upon the speakers, and gradually dilating and acquiring a strange mystic depth of expression, of which they seemed at first incapable. At these words, however, he sprang forward.

'Papa! papa! hear him! Let us both love the Lord Jesus Christ! My mother loved Him; and in the golden country of the blessed she waits for us.'

'I must go,' said the *Sah-ya* hoarsely, and attempting to rise.

'Let us pray!' said the missionary kneeling down.

The child laid his two hands together, and placing them against his forehead, bowed his head to the mat; while the father yielded to the circumstances of the case so far as to re-seat himself. Gradually, as the fervent prayer proceeded, his head drooped a little; and it was not long before he placed his elbows on his knees, and covered his face with his hands. As soon as the prayer was ended, he rose, bowed in silence, took his child by the hand, and walked away.

Day after day went by, the *Sah-ya*, as he passed the zayat, always saluting its occupant respectfully, but evincing no disposition to cultivate his acquaintance farther. He was accompanied by the boy less often than formerly; but, from casual opportunities, the missionary remarked that a strange look of thoughtfulness had crept into the childish face, softening and beautifying, though scarcely saddening it. And when occasionally the little fellow paused for a moment, to ask for a book, or exchange a word of greeting, the gay familiarity of his manner seemed to have given place to a tender, trustful affection, somewhat tinctured with awe.

Meanwhile that terrible scourge of Eastern nations, the cholera, had made its appearance, and it came sweeping through the town with its usual devastating power. Fires were kindled before every house, and kept burning night and day; while immense processions continually thronged the streets with gongs, drums, and tom-toms, to frighten away the evil spirits, and so arrest the progress of the disease. The zayat was closed for lack of visitors; and the missionary and his assistants busied themselves in attending on the sick and dying.

It was midnight when the over-wearied foreigner was roused from his slumbers by the calls of the faithful Ko Shway-bay.

'Teacher, teacher, you are wanted!'

'Where?'

The man lowered his voice almost to a whisper, but putting his hands to each side of his mouth, sent the volume of sound through a crevice in the boards. 'At the *Sah-ya's.*'

'Who?'

'I do not know, *Tsayah;* I only heard that the cholera was in the house, and the teacher was wanted, and so I hurried off as fast as possible.'

In a few minutes, the missionary had joined his assistant, and they proceeded on their way together. As they drew near the house, the Burman paused in the shadow of a bamboo hedge.

'It is not good for either of us, that we go in together; I will wait you here, *Tsayah.*'

'No, you need rest; and I shall not want you — go!'

The verandah was thronged with relatives and dependents; and from an inner room, came a wild, wailing sound which told that death was already there. No one seemed to observe the entrance of the foreigner; and he followed the sound of woe till he stood by the corpse of a little child. Then he paused in deep emotion.

'He has gone up to the golden country, to bloom forever amid the royal lilies of Paradise,' murmured a voice close to his ear.

The missionary, a little startled, turned abruptly. A middle-aged woman, holding a palm-leaf fan to her mouth, was the only person near him.

'He worshipped the true God,' she continued, suffering the individuality of her voice to glide away and mingle the wail of the mourners, and occasionally slurring a word which she dared not pronounce with distinctness; 'he worshipped the true God, and trusted in the Lord our Redeemer,—the Lord Jesus Christ, he trusted in Him. He called and he was answered, he was weary, weary and in pain; and the Lord who loved him, He took him home to be a little golden lamb in His bosom forever.'

'How long, since, did he go?'

'About an hour, *Tsayah.*' Then joining in the wail again, 'An hour amid the royal lilies; and his mother—his own beautiful mother—she of the starry eyes and silken hand——'

'Was he conscious?'

'Conscious and full of joy.'

'What did he talk of?'

'Only of the Lord Jesus Christ, whose face he seemed to see!'

'And his father?'

'His father!—Oh, my master! my noble master! he is going, too! Come and see, *Tsayah!*'

'Who sent for me?'

'Your handmaid, Sir.'

'Not the *Sah-ya?*'

The woman shook her head. 'The agony was on him—he could not have sent, if he would.'

'But how dared *you?*'

There was a look such as might have been worn by the martyrs of old upon the woman's face as she expressively answered, 'God was here!'

In the next apartment lay the fine figure of the *Sah-ya*, stretched upon a couch, evidently in the last stage of the fearful disease—his pain all gone.

'It grieves me to meet you thus, my friend,'

remarked the visitor, by way of testing the dying man's consciousness.

The *Sah-ya* made a gesture of impatience. Then his fast stiffening lips stirred, but they were powerless to convey a sound; there was a feeble movement, as though he would have pointed at something, but his half-raised finger wavered and sunk back again; and a look of dissatisfaction amounting to anxiety passed over his countenance. Finally renewing the effort, he succeeded in laying his two hands together, and with some difficulty lifted them to his forehead; and then quietly and calmly closed his eyes.

'Do you trust in Lord Gaudama in a moment like this?' inquired the missionary, uncertain for whom the act of worship was intended. There was a quick tremor in the shut lids, and the poor *Sah-ya* unclosed his eyes with an expression of mingled pain and disappointment; while the death-heavy hands slid from their position back upon the pillow.

'Lord Jesus, receive his spirit,' exclaimed the missionary solemnly.

A bright, joyous smile flitted across the face

of the dying man, parting the lips, and even seeming to shed light upon the glazed eyes; a sigh-like breath fluttered his bosom for a moment; the finger which he had before striven to lift, pointed distinctly upward, then fell heavily across his breast; and the disembodied spirit stood in the presence of its Maker.

The thrilling death-wail commenced with the departure of the breath; for although several who had been most assiduous in their attentions, glided away when it was ascertained that he who would have rewarded their fidelity was gone; there were yet many who were prevented, some by real affection, some by family pride, from so far yielding to their fears, as to withhold the honors due to the departed.

'You had better go now,' whispered the woman, 'you can do no further good, and may receive harm.'

'And who are you that you have braved the danger to yourself, of bringing me here?'

'Pass on, and I will tell you.'

They drew near the body of the child, which, by the rush to the other apartment, had been left, for a moment, alone.

'See!' said the woman, lifting the cloth reverently. A copy of the Gospel of Matthew lay on his bosom.

'Who placed it there?'

'He did, with his own dear little hand—*Amai! amai-ai!*' and the woman's voice gave expression to one swell of agony, and then died away in a low wail, like that which proceeded from the adjoining room. Presently she resumed, 'I was his mother's nurse. She got this book of you, Sir. We thought my master burned it, but he kept, and maybe studied it. Do you think that he became a true believer?'

'To whom did he *shiko* at that last moment, *Mah-aa?*'

'To the Lord Jesus Christ—I am sure of that. Do you think the Lord would receive him, Sir?'

'Did you ever read about the thief who was crucified with the Saviour?'

'Oh, yes; I read it to Moung-Moung this very day. He was holding his mother's book when the disease smote him; and he kept it in his hand, and *went up*, with it lying on his bosom. Yes, I remember.'

'The Lord Jesus Christ is just as merciful now as he was then.'

'And so they are all——oh, *'ken-payah!* it is almost too much to believe!'

'When did you first become acquainted with this religion, *Mah-aa?*'

'My mistress taught me, Sir; and made me promise to teach her baby when he was old enough; and to go to you for more instruction. But I was alone, and afraid. I sometimes got as far as the big banyan tree on the corner, and crawled away again so trembling with terror, that I could scarcely stand upon my feet. At last I found out Ko Shway-bay, and he promised to keep my secret; and he gave me books, and explained their meaning, and taught me how to pray, and I have been getting courage ever since. I should not much mind now, if they did find me out and kill me. It would be very pleasant to go up to Paradise. I think I should even like to go to-night, if the Lord would please to take me.'

It was two or three weeks before the missionary resumed his customary place in the zayat by the wayside. His hearers were scattered widely; in the neighboring jungles, in far-off towns, and in that other place from whence 'no traveller returns.'

Where was his last hopeful inquirer?

Dead.

Where the priest?

Dead.

Where the philosopher?

Fled away, none knew whither.

And the poor old water-bearer?

Dead, — died like a dog in its kennel; and but that some pitying Christian had succeeded in discovering her at the last moment, without a human witness. But, — and the missionary's heart swelled with gratitude to God as he thought of it, — there were other witnesses, nobler, tenderer, dearer to that simple, lone old creature, than all the earthly friends that ever thronged a death-bed; and these had been her bright, rejoicing convoy to the Saviour's presence.

Oh! how full of awe, how fearfully laden with the solemn interests of eternity, appeared this wondrous work of his! And how broad and clear seemed his sacred commission, as though at that moment newly traced by the finger of Jehovah!

THE END.

www.ingramcontent.com/pod-product-compliance
Lightning Source LLC
LaVergne TN
LVHW011220110826
845150LV00006B/1487

* 9 7 8 1 4 2 5 5 1 6 2 0 8 *